WITHDRAWN

A12 W9-BZL-363

ILLINOIS CENTRAL COLLEGE
HX40.R33 1965
STACKS
Democratic socialism;

A12900 660638

HX
40
.R33
1965

Radice

Democratic socialism

Illinois Central College
Learning Resource Center

PRINTED IN U.S.A.

Democratic Socialism

GILES RADICE

Democratic Socialism

A Short Survey

FREDERICK A. PRAEGER, *Publishers*

New York • Washington

Illinois Central College
Learning Resouce Center

13775

HX
40
.R33
1965

BOOKS THAT MATTER

Published in the United States of America in 1966
by Frederick A. Praeger, Inc., Publishers
111 Fourth Avenue, New York, N.Y. 10003

All rights reserved

© Giles Radice 1965

Library of Congress Catalog Card Number: 66-50707

Printed in the United States of America

To Penelope

Contents

Author's Acknowledgements

I have attempted to collect into one short book what can only be found in many. Anybody familiar with the subject will be aware how much I owe to others and also that there are over-simplifications and omissions. For this American edition I have made a number of amendments, some of which were kindly suggested by readers and reviewers of the British edition, and I have also taken the opportunity of bringing the book up to date.

To gather first-hand material, Francis Noel-Baker and I visited a number of countries during 1962 and 1963, including Germany, France, Sweden, Austria, and Israel. I would like to thank all those who helped us there, in particular officials of the Swedish Socialdemokratiska Arbetarpartiet and Lands-organisationen, the German Sozialdemokratische Partei, the Austrian Sozialistische Partei, and the Israeli Mapai and the Histadruth; and Dr Jankowitsch, Jules Moch, the late Moshe Sharett, and Ernst Wigforss.

I am grateful to Dr Shlomo Avineri, Colin Beever, Richard Gott, David Marquand, and John and Lucy Syson whose comments have much improved this book. My brother, Jonathan Radice, has throughout been an invaluable critic both on content and style. I would like to thank Miss Elizabeth Furlong for her skilful work in constructing the index and providing material for the appendix.

I am much indebted to Philip Noel-Baker who took time off from his parliamentary and other duties to make valuable suggestions as to how the book should be written.

Above all, I should like to thank Francis Noel-Baker without whose generosity, inspiration and advice this book would never have been written.

August 1966

1 Origins

This book analyses the origins, principles, and institutions of European parliamentary Socialism.[1] Though there are many variations in practice, European Socialist parties have a common approach to political problems. Democratic Socialism is used here as an umbrella term to describe the principles, policies and institutions characteristic of European parliamentary Socialism. A short definition of a Democratic Socialist—or more simply, a Socialist—is a person who believes in equality and freedom, and in the conscious, directed organisation of political, economic and social machinery to change society in accordance with these ideals.

THE INDUSTRIAL REVOLUTION

Democratic Socialism, like Communism, began as a protest against the injustices created by the industrial revolution in Europe. Today we are accustomed to continual social, economic and technological change. Few realise how recent change at this pace and on this scale is. The process of industrialisation, which has now spread to many countries, only began at the end of the eighteenth century in Britain. It brought a complete change both in man's way of life and in his expectations. In a predominantly agricultural society man was the servant of his environment. The industrial revolution gave him the machines, tools, and organisation which, if used

1 Australia, New Zealand and Israel are included in this survey of European Socialism because they share many of the political, economic and social characteristics of the European countries.

wisely, would make him its master. He could, at last, free himself from the vicious circle of poverty and build himself a society in which he could develop his own potentialities to the limit.

The British industrial revolution was the result of many factors operating together. Among the most important were the technological inventions that enabled the whole process of industrial production to be immensely speeded up. Many of these inventions were simple, or involved the combination of two existing processes which had previously been thought to be independent of each other. Yet their effect was revolutionary. The new process of reheating and purifying pig iron, invented by the Hampshire ironmaster Cort in 1783, enabled the ironmasters to concentrate the iron industry on the coal mines. Cort's invention, however, depended on the existence of a new form of power to drive his machines; this was provided by the steam engine devised by the Scottish instrument maker, James Watt, who improved the mechanism of the steam engine and adapted the piston to rotary motion. Finally the innovations of the wigmaker Arkwright and the Lancashire weaver Crompton in textile machinery, coupled with steam power, laid the basis for a power-driven textile industry. Though these discoveries did not take place until the end of the eighteenth century, they were, in fact, the result of a new attitude of mind produced by the scientific revolution over a century earlier. The scientific discoveries of two Englishmen, the astronomer, physicist and mathematician Isaac Newton, and the chemist Robert Boyle, had for the first time made men realise that scientific knowledge and hence technical invention depended on testing theories against facts.

Capital was needed to finance the production of these technological discoveries. Steady improvements in agriculture, and above all expansion in overseas trade, meant that British entrepreneurs and capitalists were able to invest in the new industries. Once again, however, the attitude of mind that made men want to invest their money, rather than spend it, was the result of new ideas about consumption which had been developed at least a century or more before.

Another important factor was the population increase—the result of a better environment and improved agricultural techniques. In the 1960s countries in Asia, Africa and South America are experiencing population explosions on a far greater scale. In the Britain of the late eighteenth and early nineteenth centuries it was the increase in population which provided the manpower to run the new factories—and also some of the consumers to buy the consumer goods, at first mostly cotton garments, that were characteristic of the British industrial revolution.

By the middle of the nineteenth century, France, Germany and the United States had begun a period of economic revolution based on railway expansion.[2] Sweden, coming comparatively late (in the 1880s) to industrial 'take-off'—or the stage when economic expansion becomes self-perpetuating—only emerged as an industrialised country at the beginning of the 1920s. In the middle of the twentieth century Russia, under the Communists, was still completing the process begun at the end of the nineteenth century under the Tsarist régime. Canada and Australia (although still offering immense potentialities) are industrialised economies like those of Western Europe. Outside Western Europe, North America, and Australasia, the drive to industrialisation is still, for the most part, only beginning. Japan alone of Asian countries has industrialised.

Yet those countries which come latest to industrialisation have the advantage of being able to use modern techniques of administration and industrial organisation to avoid some of the horrors of the earlier industrial revolutions. The evil effects were to begin with almost completely ignored by government. The architects of industrial expansion—the entrepreneurs, businessmen and capitalists—were dynamic, ruthless men who

2 For details of industrial revolutions see W. W. Rostow, *The Stages of Economic Growth*. Cambridge University Press, 1960.

believed that they should be left to get on with their own business. Their natural inclinations were reinforced by the currently fashionable economic theory—*laissez-faire*. Economists argued that 'each [man] in steadily pursuing his own aggrandisement is following that precise line of conduct which is most for the public advantage' and that there was, therefore, no need for government intervention in the economy.[3] Most Governments accepted this philosophy particularly in its application to industrial conditions and employment. The result was that, when agricultural labourers flocked to the towns created by the new industrial concentrations to escape poverty and unemployment, they found their new lives little better.

Employers had almost absolute power over their workers. Many exploited their workers in a fashion that was quite as degrading as the worst colonial oppression. At the best of times men, women, and even small children, worked inhumanly long hours for low pay in insanitary and dangerous conditions. The Children's Employment Commission Report of 1863 quotes the following piece of evidence. 'That boy of mine . . . when he was seven years old I used to carry him on my back to and fro through the snow, and he used to have to work sixteen hours a day . . . I have often knelt down to feed him as he stood by the machine, for he could not leave it or stop.' In addition, the equilibrium of the new economic system was interrupted at regular intervals by a series of economic crises and depressions. In times of depression there were a great number thrown out of work, while wages of those employed fell to below subsistence level. A British working man, describing conditions in his factory during 1842 which was one of the most severe depression years, said: 'I have seen in the factory in which I worked wives and mothers working from morning to night with only one meal; and a child brought to suck at them thrice a day. I have seen fathers of

3 *See* E. Halevy, *The Growth of Philosophical Radicalism*. Faber & Gwyer, 1928, pp. 500–1.

families coming in the morning and working till night and having only one meal, or two at the farthest extent.'

The environment in which the new urban working class worked and lived was appalling. Engels, in his *Condition of the Working Class in England,* described how in Bethnal Green, in London, it was common for a man, wife, five children and grandparents to live in a single room, where they all slept and worked. The streets of the towns were filthy and there was no drainage. The 1842 Report on the Sanitary Condition of the Labouring Population quoted the Glasgow Superintendent of Police who stated that in any large block of tenements 'I should be able to find a thousand children who have no name whatever, or only nicknames, like dogs.' In Edinburgh, the usual answer to 'When were you last washed?' was 'When I was last in prison.' There was little education and no form of recreation for the urban working class, except drink.

The result of early industrialisation, despite a slightly rising standard of living compared with pre-industrial times, was often ill health, early death, maiming and stunting of children, the break-up of the family, prostitution, drunkenness and crime. But, without political rights, the workers had no way of changing their lot.

EARLY SOCIALISTS

Some men rejected the injustices of the industrial revolution. Others even regretted the industrial revolution itself and wished to return to the pre-industrial era which they imagined as a golden age of happiness and prosperity instead of the life of endless poverty and toil it was in reality. Not all these critics were Socialists. In Britain, radicals like the journalist William Cobbett and the mob orator and Chartist leader Fergus O'Connor, enlightened businessmen like the Birmingham banker Thomas Attwood and the Rochdale industrialist John Bright, philanthropists like the aristocrat Lord Shaftesbury or even Conservative politicians like Robert Peel and

Benjamin Disraeli, were horrified by the social degradation that accompanied industrialism.

The Socialists, however, made the most rigorous criticism of the new industrial society and were concerned to change it. The word 'Socialist' was first used in 1827 by disciples of Robert Owen in the British *Co-operative Magazine* to denote a person who rejected the *laissez-faire* theory propagated by the new entrepreneur class in favour of co-operation. To the Socialists it was clear that the profit motive, left undisturbed by government action, did not and could not produce universal happiness, as the capitalists claimed. Far better to have a society based on co-operation which would, in fact, ensure fair shares for all. The apostle of co-operation, Robert Owen, born in 1771, was a highly successful member of the new entrepreneur class who owned a thriving cotton mill at New Lanark in Scotland. But he was a capitalist with a difference. He was not only a model employer who paid his employees regular wages when production was interrupted by shortage of materials during the American war; he was also a social philosopher and man of action. He saw that the employers and factory owners of the new industrial system treated their workers like beasts, and advocated, instead of the inhuman, competitive jungle of capitalism, a new system of co-operative enterprises in which the new wealth made possible by the industrial revolution might be shared by all. After trying in vain to convert his fellow factory owners and upper-class politicians, and after an unsuccessful effort to establish co-operative communities in America, he turned to the British working class. In 1834 he became president of the Grand National Consolidated Trades Union—and was the inspiration of the co-operative movement. Democratic Socialism owes a great debt to this remarkable man (see Chapter 6). In France, utopian thinkers like the commercial traveller Fourier and the aristocratic Saint-Simon also rejected the inhumanity and inefficiency of the *laissez-faire* system and advocated, instead, societies based on co-operation and planning. Saint-

Simon's solution was State control and central planning;
Fourier preferred small self-sufficient communities. All these
men, Owen, Saint-Simon, and Fourier, were Socialist—that is
to say they rejected *laissez-faire* in favour of a system where
the rewards of the new industrialism were shared by all rather
than by a few.

The most systematic, brilliant and influential Socialist
thinker of the nineteenth century was a German of Jewish
origin, Karl Marx. Marx's *Das Kapital*, one of the world's
most influential books, is a devastating analysis of the evil
effects of the Industrial Revolution. Unfortunately, having
brilliantly exposed the rigid and hypocritical theories of the
classical economists and the new business class, he put in
their place a theory of equal rigidity. For Marx claimed to be
formulating a 'science'. To Marx *Das Kapital* and his other
works were a study of the natural or scientific laws that
governed the development of human society. He boldly began
his *Communist Manifesto* with these words, 'The history of
all hitherto existing society is the history of class struggles.'
Relations between classes were determined by the factors of
production; and, according to Marx, class interests were
irreconcilable.

But Marx was only interested in past history to provide
material for his theories about the present and future. The
central fact about his theory as it applied to the present
was the inevitability of mass poverty under capitalism.
Under capitalism, there were only two classes: the capitalist
class which owned the means of production; and the working
class which owned nothing and was a mere 'appendage of
the machine'. According to Marx, the capitalist, whatever his
wishes, had to exploit the workers. For the presence of other
competing capitalists and a reserve army of unemployed
workers meant that the capitalist had to keep wages low in
order to survive in business. Yet the poverty of the workers,
which, according to Marx, could only get worse, prevented
their purchasing power keeping pace with what they produced.

The result was a series of desperate economic crises with goods accumulating for which there were no buyers.

Because Marx lived in revolutionary times, he could see no other way out of the class struggle than violent revolution. If, as Marx claimed, the state under capitalism was 'nothing more than the form of organisation which the bourgeoisie necessarily adopts both for internal and external purposes for the guarantee of its property and interests' (*German Ideology*), there was no prospect of its being used to better the workers' lot. Thus the only course open to the workers was to seize political power and establish a 'dictatorship of the proletariat'. When the workers take power, 'the expropriators are expropriated' and all the means of production, distribution and exchange are taken into State control. Marx gives little guide as to what would happen next. But he said that, by changing the old conditions of production, the workers would 'have swept away the conditions for the existence of class antagonisms and of classes generally, and will thereby have abolished its own supremacy as a class. In place of the old bourgeois society, with its classes and class antagonisms, we shall have an association in which the free development of each is the condition for the free development of all' (*Communist Manifesto*). 'From each according to his faculties, to each according to his need.' Engels, Marx's collaborator, explained the Marxist Utopia thus: 'The government of persons is replaced by the administration of things and the direction of the processes of production. The State is not abolished, it withers away' (*Anti-Duhring*).

It is little wonder that Marx's theories, with all their magnificent assurance and sweep, should have had such an influence on the generations that followed him. They offered at one and the same time a comprehensive guide to a complicated world and the certainty of deliverance from exploitation in the here and now. Today, Communist parties all over the world still believe that Marx's predictions about the development of society are correct. In fact, a short definition of a Communist is a man who still accepts the teachings of Marx. Marx's influence on Democratic Socialist parties, too, has been profound.

Marx's influence has been partly beneficial, partly pernicious. Beneficial because Marx exploded once and for all the idea that the uncontrolled forces of the market could by themselves produce a just society; pernicious because Marx claimed to be able to predict the development of society; Marx believed his work was not just a study of contemporary society but a discovery of immutable social laws. A Marxist had to accept every stage in the analysis—irreconcilable class interests, permanent mass poverty, revolution—or the whole theory came crashing to the ground. This meant that a Marxist had to wear blinkers. Though Marx never altered his unfinished masterpiece *Das Kapital* to account for changes in society, he was a profound observer of the contemporary scene. His followers have tended to shrug off awkward facts because they did not fit in with Marxist theories, and have often refused to think out the implications of changes in society.

DEMOCRACY AND THE RISE OF THE SOCIALIST PARTIES

Marx's theory ignored an extremely important political change taking place in Western Europe because it did not fit in with his theories. That change was the rise of democracy. In 1848 (the year Marx wrote *The Communist Manifesto*) an unbiased observer might well have agreed with Marx that the only way the workers could change the system was by bloody revolution. 1848 was, itself, a year of bloody and unsuccessful revolution in nearly every country in Europe—in France, Germany, Italy and Habsburg Austria. Yet, by the time Marx died in 1883, France had become a democracy; Bismarck had introduced universal suffrage in elections to the Imperial Reichstag; and Disraeli had given the vote to the British householder. Marx, himself, speaking in Amsterdam in 1872, admitted by implication that his theories had been undermined by the rise of democracy when he said, 'But we have never maintained that the way leading to that target is the same in all countries. We know that one has to take into account the institutions, mores and traditions of the different countries, and we do not deny that there do exist countries like America and England (and had I known your institutions, I would perhaps add Holland as well) where the workers are able to achieve their aims in a peaceful manner.'

The main reason for the rise in democracy was the growth of industrialism throughout Western Europe. Industry had to have educated workers. Given this fact, it was impossible in the long run to prevent the workers from forming their own associations and political parties. Contrary to Marx's predictions, the ruling classes, the aristocracy and the new business class, were intelligent enough to realise that the only way they could retain any political power was by bringing the working-classes into the political system. The 1848 revolutions failed; but they left behind them constitutions that enabled radicals and liberals to exert some influence.

One of the most interesting phenomena of the first half of the nineteenth century was the British Chartist Movement. Though almost entirely working-class in personnel and motivated by economic grievances, the Chartists' immediate objectives were political. They called for nothing less than democracy. The six points of their Charter included universal manhood suffrage, secret ballot, and payment of members. The significance of the Chartists is that they saw control of parliament as a pre-requisite of social reform. Though Chartism never had much chance of success, their ideas survived its collapse. The years of economic prosperity in Britain after 1848 saw a revival of working-class organisations—in particular the co-operatives and trade unions (see Chapter 6). The co-operative societies brought decent consumer standards to the worker. The trade unions gave him increased industrial and political bargaining power. When in the 1860s the Radical John Bright led the movement for the widening of the franchise, the organised working-class were his greatest weapon. Disraeli gave the vote to the householder in 1867, not only because he hoped to get support from the working-class, but also because he recognised that the organised working-class was the new and vital political factor. When in 1867 Bismarck gave universal manhood suffrage in the elections to the Diet of the North German Confederation he was accepting the fact that the workers had to be brought within the political system if it was to survive.

With the rise of democracy, the workers were able to form their own independent political parties to protect their own interests. It was during the last quarter of the nineteenth century that Socialism, from being a doctrine of economic and political theorists, became the creed of mass parties. The First International was little more than the talking shop of learned theoreticians and professors. The Second International was a gathering of the world's first mass political parties.[4] By 1900 there was an independent working-class party in nearly every Western European country. Many of these parties were Marxist. In 1891 the most powerful, the German Socialist party, the *Sozialdemokratische Partei Deutschlands* (SPD), which was founded in 1875, adopted a mainly Marxist programme. Its growth was rapid. With the backing of the unions, the party's popular support grew from nine per cent of the total vote in 1877 to twenty-four per cent, with three million votes and 81 seats in the German Reichstag, in 1903. The Austrian Social Democrat Party, *Sozialdemokratische Partei Öesterreichs*, now the *Sozialistische Partei Öesterreichs* (SPÖ), which drew its main strength from the German-speaking inhabitants of the Austro-Hungarian Empire, maintained close links with the SPD. The party's ideology was Marxist but because of the intellectual distinction of its leaders and theoreticians, there grew up a body of political ideas known as 'Austro-Marxism'. The French working-class movement, despite its militant tradition, was weaker in organisation than

4 *See* pp. 119–20.

the German or the Austrian. Divided into different Socialist 'sects', and including both a Marxist and a non-Marxist wing, it was briefly united in 1896—but without the whole-hearted support of the unions.

There was one working-class party which was not Marxist. That party was the *British Labour Party*. Founded in 1900 as the Labour Representation Committee, to represent the political interest of the trade unions, it took its present name in 1906. For the first few years it was mainly a trade union party pledged to safeguard trade union interests in the House of Commons. Though its secretary, Ramsay MacDonald, and the first chairman of the parliamentary party, Keir Hardie, were members of the Socialist society, the Independent Labour Party, the Labour Party did not adopt a Socialist constitution until 1918. Marx had very little influence on the British Labour Party. The trade union leaders, because they had a stake in society, were mostly pragmatic parliamentarians, and even the professed Socialists owed far more to Christian ethical principles and to the gradualist philosophy of the Fabian Society[5] than to the teachings of Marx. Up to 1914 the Labour Party was forced to work with the Liberal Government in Parliament because the Labour group was small (with only 42 M.P.s to the 272 Liberals) and because they feared the reactionary Conservative opposition. Yet Labour's support was increasing rapidly in the industrial areas, while there were four million workers affiliated to the Trades Union Congress. There was a good chance therefore that they would come to power by constitutional means.

There were other Socialist parties, which, though they still clung to Marxist doctrines, had begun to abandon Marxism in practice. The most important in this group, which included the Scandinavian and Belgian parties, was the Swedish

5 The Fabian Society, founded in 1883 by Beatrice and Sydney Webb and Bernard Shaw, was and is a small but influential society of Socialist intellectuals who devote themselves to research and believe in the establishment of Socialism by parliamentary means.

Social-Democratic Labour Party (*Socialdemokratiska arbetar-partiet*). This was founded in 1889 by the trade unions and took the German Social Democrats as a model. Its goal was to be the establishment of a classless society through the socialisation of the means of production. Yet in 1889 the party congress passed a resolution which rejected any in-sinuation that 'we, because we are still not fully supported by the people, intend to risk the very existence of the labour movement by a violent upheaval'. Already by 1914 the Swedish Social Democrats and trade unions had had a con-siderable influence on events. An important factor in the progressive and peaceful passage of the Swedish industrial revolution, which followed those of most of the larger European countries, was the strength of the working-class movement. The Swedish Social Democrats also had a decisive effect in widening the franchise. In 1902 they called a political strike which forced the Swedish parliament to recognise the principle of universal manhood suffrage. In 1907 the Social Democrats, in alliance with the Liberals, forced limited parliamentary reform on the Second House of the Swedish parliament. By 1915 the Social Democrats, after a phenomenally swift advance, had become the largest party in the Second House.

The new opportunities afforded by the rise of democracy influenced even the most orthodox of the Marxist Socialist parties, the German Social Democrats. Inside that party there had been considerable argument about the relevance of Marxist doctrine to conditions in Germany. Some German Socialists, among them the brilliant theoretician Eduard Bernstein, supported by the trade union leaders, demanded that Marxist teaching and theory should be brought up to date in the light of new conditions. Bernstein pointed out that the position of the workers was improving rather than deteriorating, and that the increased power of the working-classes, through their parliamentary and trade union repre-sentatives, made it a probability that the workers could bring about the classless society in a gradualist and constitutional manner.[6] Unfortunately the Social Democrat leaders compromised: while accepting parliamentary democracy and evolutionary methods in practice, they remained committed to Marxist theory of revolution.

Even more unhappily the German Social Democrats, through their dominance over the Second International, forced their 'dogmatism' on to other parties at a time when there were opportunities in their countries, particularly in France, for the emergence of a genuine Democratic Socialism. Some leading French Socialists, including the great Socialist leader, thinker and orator Jean Jaurès, argued that democracy was an essential part of Socialism and should be defended at all costs, even if that meant co-operation with the bourgeois parties. Other French Socialists, including the Marxist Jules Guesde, replied that this policy was in effect a betrayal of working-class interests. This quarrel among the French Socialists had arisen over the Dreyfus case, which had led to the French Republic and democratic institutions being attacked by the forces of the Right. At the 1904 Amsterdam Congress of the Second International, which devoted most of its discussions to this particular problem, the powerful German Social Democrat delegation voted Jaurès down. In 1905 the two opposing French groups made up their quarrel and united on the basis of the Amsterdam decision to form the *Section Française de l'Internationale Ouvrière* (SFIO). The price paid for French Socialist unity was the loss of a great opportunity for developing a democratic Socialism applicable to France where, in contrast to Germany, there was responsible parliamentary democracy.

By 1914, the Socialist parties and their trade union allies had become a power in Europe. Though the Socialists had not yet formed a government, the German Social Democrats were the largest party in the Reichstag, while the Swedish Social Democrats became the largest party in the Second

6 See E. Bernstein, *Evolutionary Socialism*. Socialist Library, 1909.

House of the Swedish parliament a year later. Socialist and trade union pressure was pushing non-Socialist politicians into making social reforms. In Britain a Liberal government, conscious of the new Labour Party breathing down its neck, had introduced a series of reforms, including the first health and unemployment insurance scheme, a national network of labour exchanges, and a law protecting the trade unions. Nearly twenty years earlier, the German Chancellor Bismarck had tried unsuccessfully to pre-empt the rising power of the Social Democrats by himself introducing the first State social insurance scheme. Outside Europe, the *Australian Labour Party* formed a minority government in 1904—the first Labour or Socialist government in the world—and a majority Labour government (1910–13) brought in pensions for invalids and maternity allowances. But in spite of their very real achievements, the thinking of Socialist leaders was still confused. While conditions in most of Europe, except Tsarist Russia, gave Socialist parties a chance to achieve power by democratic means, many Socialists still clung to Marx's outdated revolutionary theories. Devotion to Marxist theories was rapidly becoming a substitute for independent analysis or action. For example, the German Social Democrats, the most powerful Socialist party in the world, gave little thought as to how they were to make the Reichstag more powerful or what they would do if they actually achieved office.

THE 1914–18 WAR AND THE RUSSIAN REVOLUTION
The Socialists cannot be blamed for not being able to prevent the 1914–18 war. The simple but tragic fact was that they did not have the power to prevent it. At successive meetings of the International, unanimous resolutions were passed condemning war as a form of capitalist aggression. But without power over the military machines there was very little they could do to prevent war other than pass resolutions.[7] In fact, when war finally came in August 1914, the French, German and

7 *See* pp. 120–1.

Austrian Socialist parties, after strong initial protests, voted
for war credits. Once there was no chance of avoiding war it
became a question of national defence. The Austrian Social
Democrat leader, Adler, himself German speaking, put the
dilemma for the powerless Socialists all over Europe in these
words, 'An incomprehensible German to have done anything
else (than vote for war credits). An incomprehensible Social
Democrat to have done it without being racked with pain,
without a hard struggle with himself and all his feelings.' In
the heat of a war (which they had done their best to prevent)
nationality triumphed over working-class solidarity.

Paradoxically the first World War, in spite of the terrible
human suffering it brought with it, did, in fact, strengthen
the position of the working-class. In order to win the war, the
ruling classes had to pay attention to the welfare and morale
of their soldiers and citizens. Every able-bodied man had to
fight—and an enemy bullet was no respecter of classes or
persons. There had also to be some attempt at sharing food
fairly among citizens if the war was to be kept going. In most
of the countries at war the political leaders took Socialists
and trade union leaders into their confidence to ensure that
the munitions factories worked smoothly. In 1914 the old
French Marxist Jules Guesde joined the French cabinet and
Vandervelde joined the Belgian cabinet. In Germany, the
Socialists agreed to an 'electoral' truce in the Reichstag. In
Britain Arthur Henderson, Leader of the Labour Party, was
a member of both Asquith's and Lloyd George's governments.
The experience of office and responsibility gained during the
war by Socialist leaders immensely strengthened the Socialist
electoral impact when the people, sickened by war, turned
to the Left. The war discredited the old leaders, and the
peoples of Europe began to look to the Socialists as the natural
alternatives. The rash of Socialist governments that appeared
after the war all over Europe—in Sweden the first Socialist
Prime Minister, in Austria a Socialist Chancellor, in Weimar
Germany, primarily the creation of the Social Democrats, a

Social Democrat President and Chancellor and subsequent S.P.D. participation in later coalitions, and in Britain the two minority Labour governments of 1924 and 1929–31 owed much to the 1914–18 war.

The other decisive change brought about by the war was the Russian Revolution. The war destroyed the Tsarist régime's crumbling authority. In March 1917, in face of unrest caused by the severe war casualties and by economic hardship, the Tsar abdicated.

There were two main Russian Socialist parties—the Socialist Revolutionaries and the Social Democratic party. The Russian Social Democratic party, founded in 1898, was a member of the Second International, as were the two successor parties, the Bolsheviks and the Mensheviks. The Bolsheviks, so known because they were the majority faction when the Russian Social Democrats split in 1903, were led by the Marxist intellectual Vladimir Ilyitch Ulianov, better known as Lenin. Lenin made the Bolshevik Party quite different from the other parties in the International. He had broken with the Mensheviks, or minority faction, because he believed a proletarian revolution could only be led by a disciplined, ruthless, conspiratorial sect of revolutionaries fulfilling the Marxist role of 'dictatorship of the proletariat', not by a democratic mass party on the lines of the German Social Democrats. Lenin believed, too, that revolution would not come of itself but would have to be initiated by the Party. Lenin's case was strengthened by political conditions in Russia. The autocratic Tsarist government could, in the short run, only be overturned by force. The war gave Lenin his chance. From the first, he denounced the war as a bourgeois imperialist struggle for markets and plunder, but, at the same time, he saw that war could lead to proletarian revolution all over Europe. When the weakening of the Russian war effort led to the abdication of the Tsar, Lenin and the Bolsheviks played brilliantly on the weakness of the new Provisional Government and added deliberately to the general confusion by calling for a transfer of power to the Soviets of Workers' and Soldiers' Deputies, which had sprung up in the towns and at the front. Gaining the support of the workers in the big cities and of some of the soldiers through their exploitation of the great issues of peace, bread, and land, the Bolsheviks seized power in November.

The nature of the new Communist régime, as it came to be called, was shaped by conditions in Russia. The basic economic fact about Russia was that it was still an agricultural country. In 1914 Russia was the least advanced industrially of the major European nations. It was a queer paradox that the only successful Communist revolution that followed the war should happen not in industrially advanced Germany, as Marx foretold, but in backward Russia. But this meant that Lenin and the Bolsheviks were not likely to gain the support of the peasants, to whom the idea of agricultural collectivisation was anathema. In the last free election at the end of November 1917, the peasant party par excellence, the Social Revolutionaries, had twice the amount of support received by the Bolsheviks. The basic political fact about Russia was that it was accustomed to being ruled from above. If one considers too the existence of a hostile world beyond Russia's frontiers and Lenin's own preference for a conspiratorial, disciplined revolutionary party, it is not surprising that the Communist régime soon degenerated into that totalitarian one-party rule with complete and ruthless control over all the arms of the State, the judiciary, the Press, and all independent institutions, so characteristic of the Stalinist era.

The reaction of Socialists to the Russian Revolution was, at first, wildly enthusiastic. Even the British Labour Party leaders welcomed it. After a time, however, disillusionment set in. Socialists objected to the harsh and dictatorial methods of the Communists. The great philosopher Bertrand Russell, after a visit to Russia in 1920, wrote, 'I am compelled to reject Bolshevism for two reasons. First, because the price mankind must pay to achieve Communism by Bolshevik methods is too terrible; and secondly because, even after paying the price, I do not believe the result would be what the Bolsheviks profess to desire.' The Berne International Conference of Socialists of 1919 passed a resolution which specifically condemned Bolshevism as a model for Socialist parties. 'A reorganised society more and more permeated with Socialism cannot be realised, much less permanently established, unless it rests upon the triumphs of Democracy and is rooted in the principles of liberty.'

This split on principle between Socialists and Communists was mirrored by a similar split in organisation. The Communists sought to establish, in place of the old International which had collapsed in 1914, a new centralised International committed to international revolution and based on Moscow. They therefore deliberately divided the Socialist movement. They received some support: in France the Communists outvoted the Socialists at the Tours meeting of the French Socialist Party, thus capturing the party machinery; while sizeable Communist parties were established in Germany and Italy. The European Socialist parties, after one group had attempted to mediate with the Communist International, then formed a separate Labour and Socialist International in 1923. Thus the breach between those who believed Socialism could be established by democratic means and those who believed only in revolutionary Socialism was formalised. In 1923 Democratic Socialism emerged for the first time as a separate and independent political philosophy —though not yet as a viable one.

THE WORLD ECONOMIC CRISIS AND THE EMERGENCE OF A VIABLE DEMOCRATIC SOCIALISM

The causes of the 1939–45 war are complex: there are the questions of the validity of the Versailles Peace settlement, the personality of Hitler, German militarism, and the weakness and indecision of the leaders of France and Britain to be considered. But one fact stands out—the mass-unemployment

of the 1930s. How could the intricate structure of post-war
Europe and the new and fragile Weimar Republic of Germany
be expected to survive when in January 1932 there were six
million Germans registered as unemployed?

The Great Depression, as the economic crisis that caused
the mass unemployment was called, finally killed the capitalist
myth. All through the 1920s right-wing politicians and business leaders argued that the capitalist system, if left to
itself, would, in some unexplained way, ensure that everybody received a fair deal. Unemployment they dismissed as a
natural phenomenon. The most literal exponent of this creed
was the Republican President of the United States, Calvin
Coolidge, who believed that it was his job as President to do
as little as possible. He blandly assured the American people
that 'the chief business of government is business', and that
'the government can remedy the economic ills of the people
more by a system of rigid economy in public expenditure
than can be accomplished through any other action'. Even
during the prosperous 1920s it was difficult to argue that the
capitalist system resulted in fair shares when in Britain, for
example, 5 per cent of the population owned nearly 80 per
cent of the property. The Great Depression of the 1930s
finally put paid, as well, to the idea that the unregulated
capitalist system was efficient. By 1933, 30 per cent of the
German and American labour force and 22 per cent of British
workers were unemployed.

The Communists welcomed the Great Depression. It
seemed, at last, to bear out Marx's predictions that the world
was on the eve of a great proletarian revolution. They were
able to point to the contrast between the mass-unemployment
of the Western democracies and the purposive planning that
Stalin had begun in Soviet Russia. In reality, of course, Russia
faced a different problem. Whereas the dilemma facing the
United States, Britain, Germany, France and Sweden was how
to ensure the smooth running of an industrialised economy,
the Russian task was to transform a backward one. The Com-

munists also hid the heavy cost in human lives that their policy
of forced industrialisation involved. Even so, many Europeans began to despair of a solution to the problem of mass-
unemployment within a democratic framework; and some
turned to Communism and even to Nazism for an answer.

Certainly there was cause to despair. Right-wing politicians
had no answer to unemployment except to pursue a policy
of rigid government economy, which by cutting back investment and purchasing power even further made unemployment
worse. The Great Depression had brought down Socialist
governments in Germany and Britain as well. The German
Social Democrats, who had been the architects of Germany's
first responsible parliamentary régime and were in power
when the Depression struck Germany, had no practical
answer to it. Fritz Tarnow, the German trade unionist, put
their dilemma in these words: 'Are we sitting at the sickbed
of capitalism, not only . . . as doctors who want to cure the
patient, but also as cheerful heirs who cannot wait for the
end and would like to hasten it with poison? . . . This double
role, doctor and heir, is a damned difficult task.' As true
Marxists, all the Social Democrats had to do was to wait to
inherit their kingdom; as practical Socialists in office with a
Socialist Prime Minister, Müller, they wanted to relieve the
workers' conditions. In fact they had the worst of both
worlds. On the one hand, they diminished purchasing power
by cutting back government spending, balancing the budget
and maintaining the gold value of the mark; on the other
hand, because they refused to agree to cuts in unemployment
benefits, they resigned and so brought down the coalition
government which proved to be the last parliamentary government of the ill-fated Weimar Republic. There is little doubt
that the failure of the Social Democrats made Hitler's path to
power easier.

In Britain, the second minority Labour government, led by
Ramsay MacDonald, was destroyed by the economic crisis.
Ramsay MacDonald, who knew little about economics,

ignored the advice of brilliant economists like Keynes and of the trade union leader Ernest Bevin, and relied instead on orthodox *laissez-faire* economic advisers, who advocated a deflationary policy of government economy. When a minority of the Cabinet, as well as the leading trade unionists, refused to accept the cut in unemployment benefits demanded by New York bankers as part of the price of a loan to keep Britain on the gold standard, MacDonald resigned and formed a new coalition government of Conservatives and Liberals. The Labour Party refused to follow its leader and went into opposition, where it remained, powerless to influence events, until 1940.

Democratic Socialist hopes were kept alight, however, by the success of Socialist governments in two smaller countries. In 1937 Clement Attlee, then leader of the British Labour opposition, wrote in glowing terms of the achievements of the Swedish Social Democratic government of 1932–36 and the New Zealand Labour government which came to power in 1935, 'Sweden has afforded perhaps the most remarkable example of the successful development of Socialism through constitutional means that is to be found in Europe... This last year, however, has afforded by far the most interesting development in constitutional Socialism that we have yet seen. I refer, of course, to the work of the newly elected Labour government in New Zealand.'

When in 1931 the number of unemployed in Sweden began to assume massive proportions, the Swedish Social Democrats, then in opposition, carefully worked out, with the help of their economic expert Ernst Wigforss and a number of brilliant economists of the 'Stockholm School', a radical programme, involving massive government intervention, to fight unemployment and stimulate recovery throughout the economy. The Social Democrats fought the 1932 elections on this programme; polled over 40 per cent of the votes cast; and increased their representation from 90 to 104 seats in the Lower House of Parliament, thus reducing the anti-

Social Democrat majority in that House to only six. The Social Democrat leader, Per Albin Hansson, was therefore called upon to form a minority government, but his hand was strengthened by the informal parliamentary support he received from the Agrarian Party. While the Weimar régime was collapsing in Germany, the Swedish Social Democrats set about solving the unemployment problem. Their measures (which are described in detail in Chapter 3) included a nation-wide system of public works financed by loan to provide work and to stimulate general economic recovery; special aids to agriculture to restore agricultural purchasing power; and an ambitious beginning to a fully-fledged system of social services to underpin the economy with a cushion of social security. And they succeeded: the number of unemployed fell from 189,225 in January 1933 to 9,600 in 1937.

In Australasia, the Australian Labour government was brought down by the Depression and party splits. But the *New Zealand Labour Party* won a landslide victory in 1935. The New Zealand Labour Government, with Michael Savage as first Labour Prime Minister, took immediate steps to bring about economic recovery. These comprised an expanded public works programme including roads, hydro-electric enterprises and public buildings, promotion of secondary industries, and a system of guaranteed prices for dairy produce. Employment was also promoted by the extension of the forty-hour week in place of the normal forty-four hour week. Control of credit was ensured by the nationalisation of the Reserve Bank. The result of the government's economic policies was a remarkable expansion of employment. Whereas in 1935 the number of unemployed was 60,806, by June 1938 there were only 8,721 unemployed. By the 1938 Social Security Act the Labour government introduced the most ambitious social services the world had ever seen; these included the first health service, family allowances, unemployment and sickness benefits and old age pensions. It also introduced rent control and embarked on a vigorous housing programme.

The work of the two governments—Labour in New Zealand, Social Democrat in Sweden—proved conclusively that Democratic Socialism was a practical proposition. Not only had they showed that a determined democratic government could solve the unemployment problem; they had also showed that it was possible through a comprehensive system of social security to create a far more equalitarian society. The only comparable achievement was that of Roosevelt's Democratic administration in the United States. It is true that American problems were on a far larger scale. Yet Roosevelt's 'New Deal', as it was called, was less well thought out or coherent than the programmes of New Zealand Labour or the Swedish Social Democrats; and its results were relatively less impressive. In 1940 there were still eight million unemployed in the United States. There was a brief moment when it seemed as though Blum's Socialist-led Popular Front government might succeed in reforming French society and unifying a divided nation. Unfortunately, Blum's government, weakened by the refusal of the Communists to join it, was destroyed by the blindness of the Radicals. The post-war Socialist and left-wing reforms which were to change the lives of most Western Europeans owed most to the pioneering work of the two successful Socialist administrations of the 1930s.

There was another lesson to be learnt from the experience of the depression years. The failure of the Social Democrats in Germany and Austria showed that mastery of Marxist dialectic was more of a handicap than a help to Democratic Socialists in power or with the chance of power. The failure of MacDonald's Labour government proved that orthodox Conservative thinking was equally irrelevant. The only Socialist governments who were successful were those who discarded old shibboleths. If it is to be successful, a Socialist government, above all other democratic governments, needs to be receptive to new ideas and courageous enough to act on them.

2 Principles

While Democratic Socialists do not have a holy book of words, they have always believed that political action must be based on carefully defined principles. Man's behaviour, in politics as in everyday life, is governed by his assumptions and beliefs. The most 'natural' action is, in fact, only the result of thought and constant practice. So-called 'hard-headed realists', who deny the importance of principles, are just lazy thinkers who have not troubled to work out their own assumptions or those whose assumptions are too sinister to bear public scrutiny. It was Disraeli, the unorthodox British Conservative politician and statesman, who defined a realist as 'he who can be depended upon to perpetuate the mistakes of his ancestors'.

The early Socialists criticised nineteenth-century industrial society because they thought it unjust. Even Marx, who claimed that his critique of society was entirely scientific, used words like 'exploitation' in a highly emotive way. In the same way, when Bebel and Bernstein in Germany, Branting and Hansson in Sweden, Jaurès and Blum in France, Henderson and Attlee in Britain, led the parliamentary advance of Socialism, their policies were designed to put right the injustices that had horrified Marx and Owen. In other words, when these men criticised society, they criticised it from the standpoint of certain assumptions about what was right and wrong. Because they believed in individual equality and freedom, they were against the exploitation of one man by another; and they wished, through the conscious and purposive use of collective action to develop society towards greater equality and freedom for all.

Now, as then, the basis of Democratic Socialism is its insistence on the importance of the individual and the recognition that his rights and opportunities can often only be protected and enhanced by collective decisions. The abstract concepts of equality and freedom assume concrete reality only when translated into individual terms. The 1962 Oslo Declaration of the Socialist International says, 'We Democratic Socialists proclaim our conviction that the ultimate aim of political activity is the fullest development of every human personality.'

Every human being has different skills, abilities, potentialities and tastes; but Democratic Socialists believe that these individual differences are negligible by comparison with our common humanity—an ideal which Christians share though not all their religious leaders have been concerned to apply it to everyday life. If every individual is important, exploitation of one man by another must be wrong. This is why Robert Owen wrote with such horror of workers' conditions in early industrial Britain. 'I soon discovered with what care lifeless machines are treated and with what neglect machines which are alive.' This is why Socialists rejected British oppression in Ireland, Tsarist tyranny in Imperial Russia, and Stalinist rule in Eastern Europe, and today reject Portuguese colonialism in Angola, and white domination in South Africa. Because individual rights, not the rights of party, class, race or nation are the most important, Socialists reject the concepts of class rule and class war, and abhor any kind of racialism.

A belief in the importance of the individual and, following on from that, a belief in individual freedom and equality and the application of these principles to society unite all Democratic Socialists. The Oslo Declaration says: 'To us, both freedom and equality are precious and essential to human happiness. They are the twin pillars upon which the ideal of human brotherhood rests.' These principles were not invented by Socialists. Long ago the philosophers of Ancient Greece had discussed the relation between the state and the individual, and analysed the concepts of freedom and equality. The watchwords of the French Revolution were '*Liberté, Egalité, Fraternité*'. But the gap between discussion and practice was a wide one. In Ancient Greece 80 to 90 per cent of the population (the women and slaves) had no rights at all; while the French Revolution ended in a welter of bloodshed and military reaction. Only in the nineteenth century, with the new conditions and opportunities of the industrial society, did the concepts of equality and freedom lose their abstract qualities; only when Socialists had devised political, economic and social machinery to put these principles into effect, did they become practical political objectives.

By the validity of these two principles—individual equality and freedom—and by the effectiveness of their practical application, Democratic Socialism stands or falls. The validity of these principles, as opposed to their practical application, does not depend on empirical evidence—that is to say evidence based on experience and fact. Not that there is any lack of good empirical reasons why every man and woman should be both free and equal. Societies without freedom and equality—like South Africa or some of the Communist countries—are usually racked by political discord or class dissension as well as being corrupt and inefficient. But the basic objection to oppression and inequality is that every man and woman is entitled to enjoy freedom and equality as of right.

There can be no freedom without equality or equality without freedom. As the Swedish Social Democrat programme of 1960 says, 'There is no conflict between freedom and equality; on the contrary they are interdependent.' There cannot be freedom for all unless everybody enjoys it equally. If freedom is a privilege of the few, then in the words of the famous British Socialist philosopher and historian, R. H. Tawney, 'Freedom for the strong is oppression for the weak.' Since the black African does not share equality—political, social and economic—with the white man, South Africa is not a free country. But equal social, economic and political rights are a sham without freedom to enjoy them. On paper the Russian

Constitution of 1936, devised by Stalin, was one of the most advanced in the world, with freedom of speech and assembly, independence of the judiciary, and equal economic and social rights. Yet *Pravda*, the official organ of the Communist Party, put the constitution in its true light when it commented on the constitution in its issue of 22 June 1936, 'We shall not give a scrap of paper nor an inch of room for those who think differently [from the Party]...'; while the standard Russian history of the Soviet judicial system has this to say of the independence of judiciary, 'It must be borne in mind that the independence of the judges and their subordination only to the law does not mean independence from the state, or independence from the policy of the party and the government, for the court is an organ of power, and its function is one of the functions of state control.'

EQUALITY

Words like 'equality' and 'freedom' are falling into disrepute: partly because they are used so often by politicians of a bewildering variety of political parties, creeds and nationalities, that they have become almost meaningless; partly because so many evil things have been done in their name.

Let us examine how these words are used by Democratic Socialists. No one supposes that every man is born with equal abilities; what Socialists believe is that every human being is worthy of equal consideration. In the words of the Swedish Social Democrat programme of 1960, 'Social Democratic ideas have their deepest roots in the integrity and basic equality of all human beings.' From this it follows that every man should be given an equal opportunity throughout life to develop his own talents and live his own life in the manner he thinks best. The Swedish programme adds, 'Equal opportunities must first and foremost mean the right and opportunity of all to develop according to their inclinations and ability.'

What are the implications of this concept of equality? It does not mean literally identical material circumstances, but that

differences within narrow limits should be no greater than are
strictly necessary to call forth those special efforts, talents,
sacrifices and resources without which a community cannot
progress at its maximum capacity to the general benefit of all.
Few Socialists (except the Irish playwright Bernard Shaw)
have believed that it was either fair or practical for every man
to have a precisely equal income. Different people have different needs and desires. A man with a larger family obviously
needs a larger income than a man with a small family; one man
might choose to increase his leisure while another might prefer
to continue working to save up money for the future. It would
be unfair, and probably harmful to the community, if special
gifts, abilities and qualifications, used in a way that is helpful
to society, were not rewarded appropriately. But any difference
must not be larger than is socially justified. Wide variations in
wealth are indefensible because they are unjust as well as
causing class divisions and hatred. This applies not only within
a single country but between nations as well. Extremes of
wealth between the peoples of the countries of the West and
the peoples of countries in Asia and Africa are just as wrong as
extreme differences between citizens of an individual country.
The tragic and growing difference of wealth between Americans and Western Europeans on the one hand, and, say,
Indians, Tanzanians and Bolivians on the other, is morally
indefensible as well as dangerous for the peace and prosperity of the world. The Socialist International in its Oslo
Declaration of 1962 committed all Socialist parties to do their
utmost to get rid of these inequalities of wealth between
nations.

In addition to real material equality, Democratic Socialists
lay emphasis on equality of status. This does not just mean
'equality of opportunity'—a slogan which is now often on the
lips of Conservatives. 'Equality of opportunity' may mean
nothing more than an equal opportunity to be vastly unequal
both in the economic and social sphere. The American Declaration of Independence of 1776 says, 'We hold these truths to

be self-evident: that all men are created equal, that they are endowed by their Creator with certain inalienable rights; that among these are life, liberty, and the pursuit of happiness.' Theoretically, American society, through its nominally egalitarian educational system, offers every American an equal chance in life (though, in fact, Negroes and poor whites get worse educational opportunities than other sections of the community); but in spite of the educational system, there is extreme economic and social inequality. In 1955 the one-tenth of the population with the lowest incomes received after tax about 1 per cent of the total money income of the country, while the tenth with the highest incomes received 27 per cent of the total income. In 1954, though only 3 per cent of all families had incomes after tax of more than £5,000, they received 15·5 per cent of the total income.[1] Nearly 20 per cent of the population live, by American standards, on the edge of poverty; while the Negroes, in spite of progressive civil rights legislation, are still very much second-class citizens. 'Equality of opportunity' is certainly one of the prerequisites of social equality. But it can lead to a society where the prizes go to the strong, and the weak are left to fend for themselves. In other words, 'equality of opportunity' can be used to justify a society in which very great inequalities exist.

Democratic Socialists reject this definition of equality of opportunity. They assert that unless all children really share the same educational opportunities, 'equality of opportunity' is merely an empty phrase. As the 1959 Bad Godesburg programme of the German Social Democrats puts it, 'All privileged access to educational institutions must be abolished.' But equal educational opportunities does not just mean having an equal chance to go to the best schools. It also means that a child should not be handicapped during his schooling, as are American Negroes and poor whites, by living in a slum or in a home dominated by poverty. For most impartial experts now agree that intelligence is not solely a question of heredity; it

1 See J. K. Galbraith, The Affluent Society. Hamish Hamilton, 1958.

is also shaped by environment. If this is so, 'equality of opportunity' only has meaning in a society which already has a high degree of equality—in income distribution, in social security and health services, and in housing.[2] Recent studies of European education (for example the British Robbins report) show that many more people than previously suspected are capable of benefiting from some form of advanced education. If this is so, then any *élite* theory of education with prizes for the few will not only be morally wrong but also wasteful and frustrating in practice.

Basing 'equality of opportunity' entirely on intelligence is, in any case, unfair. Long ago Marx pointed out that, as men are differently endowed, equality when measured by any single standard must lead to unequal rewards. In his book *The Future of Socialism*, the British Labour economist and politician C. A. R. Crosland stated that 'it was the injustice of isolating, as a basis for extreme inequality, certain selected ones out of the multiple strands that go to make up the human personality, which constitutes the fundamental ethical case against any élite or aristocracy'. Ideally every child should have an equal chance of developing its interests and personality regardless of measured intelligence—and this could mean giving more education to the subnormal than to the brilliant child.

In any case, 'equality of opportunity' is not enough, whether it is based on intelligence, character, or anything else. A society based solely on rewards—social as well as financial—for the stronger members of the community would be the negation of equality. The sick, the aged, the unemployed, the weak, the lonely, the poor, the exploited and the unlucky, deserve special treatment. Any doctrine of equality that excludes any section of society is partial and unfair. As Tawney puts it, 'So the doctrine which throws all its emphasis on the importance of opening avenues to the individual

2 *See* C. A. R. Crosland, *The Conservative Enemy*, Cape, 1962, for a fuller discussion of this point.

advancement is partial and one-sided. It is right in insisting on the necessity of opening a free career to aspiring talent; it is wrong in suggesting that opportunities to rise, which can, of their nature, be seized only by the few, are a substitute for a general diffusion of the means of civilisation, which are needed by all men, whether they rise or not, and which those who cannot climb the economic ladder and who sometimes, indeed, do not desire to climb, may turn to as good account as those who can.'[3]

Critics of Socialism often argue that social equality means uniformity. This is quite untrue. The whole point about the Socialist concept of equality is to give *every* man and woman the opportunity to make his or her life more varied and interesting in the way he or she thinks best. Those who criticise equality on the grounds that it will lead to dullness and uniformity are usually people whose lives are already full and varied and who do not think it possible for others less fortunate than themselves to share their opportunities. Socialists do not want to make life dull and drab but to extend the opportunities of a full and varied life so that these can be shared by all. In the words of the 1951 Frankfurt Declaration of the Socialist International 'Socialism means far more than a new economic and social system. Economic and social progress have moral value to the extent that they serve to liberate and develop the human personality.'

FREEDOM

The second great Democratic Socialist ideal is freedom of the individual. In his book *The Labour Party in Perspective*, Clement Attlee, the former British Labour Prime Minister, wrote: 'The aim of Socialism is to give greater freedom to the individual.' Without freedom, equality is meaningless. Indeed the whole point of equality is to ensure that everybody gets his share of freedom.

Freedom does not, of course, mean licence. It does not mean

3 R. H. Tawney, *Equality*. Allen and Unwin, 1952 edition. p. 113.

freedom to kill, steal, oppress, or in any way deprive others of their freedom. It means rather the opportunity to exercise individual choice and responsibility; to live one's own life in one's own way to the limit which equal respect for other people's freedom permits.

The role of government is to protect this individual freedom —not to invade it. How individual freedom is enjoyed, so long as it is not at the expense of others, should not be dictated by politics or politicians. It is here that Socialists disagree most widely with Communists. Communists denounce freedom, as it is practised in democratic countries, as a bourgeois façade masking the exploitation of the masses by the ruling class; and, as the Communist Party claims to be the only interpreter of the wishes of the masses, there is no activity in Communist countries where the Party's decision is not final. In theory at least, only the Communist Party can enjoy freedom.

The great change in Russia and in East European countries like Hungary and Poland since the death of Stalin is that some sections of the community, particularly the technicians and scientists, are now permitted in certain limited spheres to criticise those in authority. The emergence of a large number of well-educated, critically minded citizens meant that communist leaders had to curb some of the most notorious and obnoxious activities of the party. Once the sphere of personal freedom has been widened in this way, it is difficult to stop future advances.

If the role of government is to protect individual freedom, then it must necessarily also protect political freedom. Political freedom implies certain rights such as free choice of government, freedom of speech in private and public (including freedom to demonstrate), above all the freedom to criticise the government and to organise opposition to it with a view to replacing it. For Democratic Socialists all these political rights are essential to freedom. That is why they condemned Stalin's Russia and Hitler's Germany, and now denounce Salazar's Portugal, and Verwoerd's South Africa.

There are good, sound, practical arguments, as well as moral ones, for political freedom, especially the freedom to criticise. Without freedom to criticise established scientific theories, religious dogmas, social conventions and political institutions, society is unlikely to better itself very fast. Bertrand Russell has said 'Almost all the progress in the world from the earliest times is attributable to science and the scientific temper.'[4] Milovan Djilas, then Vice-President of Yugoslavia, writing in the Party paper *Borba* before he was imprisoned, said, 'Every restriction of freedom of thought or opinion, even if made for a splendid ideology, must inevitably lead to the corruption of those responsible for it.' It is sometimes argued that dictatorships are always more efficient than democracies. But no democratic leader was more incompetent than Mussolini who spent eighteen years preparing for war. Yet when war came in 1940 Italy was worse equipped than she had been in 1915.[5] Hitler led his country to disastrous defeat which resulted in the partition of Germany. Stalin's efforts to increase agricultural productivity resulted in famine. Because dictators usually dislike criticism, they often make monumental blunders which democratic leaders avoid. The freedom to criticise is a spur to efficiency.

Other democratic parties share the Democratic Socialist belief in safeguarding the basic political freedoms. The special contribution of Socialists to the concept of freedom is their conviction that it is the government's task not only to preserve political freedoms, but to widen the frontiers of freedom as a whole. The British Labour Prime Minister, Harold Wilson, has written: 'While we yield to none in our determination to fight for the basic political freedoms ... we believe that no man is truly free who is in economic thraldom, who is the slave to unemployment, or economic insecurity, or the crippling cost of medical treatment, who lacks opportunities

4 Bertrand Russell, *Theory and Practice of Bolshevism.* Unwin Books, 1962. p. 55.
5 A. J. P. Taylor, *Politics in Wartime.* Hamish Hamilton, 1964. p. 196.

in both the material and the priceless immaterial scope to a fuller life and the fullest realisation of his talents and abilities.'[6] It is the government's duty to ensure that every member of the community is prosperous. This is fundamental. When a man is poor and hungry, he concentrates on survival—as in Asia, Africa and most of South America today. When he is more prosperous, money and increased leisure give him opportunities to develop his personality in his own way. Further, though 'affluence' does not automatically produce an upsurge of civic consciousness, poverty makes it more difficult for a man to play a part in the community. *Poverty limits choice; prosperity extends it.*

Widening freedom also implies that the government should be responsible for providing citizens with opportunities to widen their experience. The Frankfurt Declaration of the Socialist International says 'Socialism seeks to give all men the means to raise their cultural standard and foster the creative aspirations of the human spirit.' For example a progressive government must not only build schools and nurseries; it must also provide radio and television services, theatres, museums, art galleries, opera houses, sports centres, national parks and so on. A government should also be responsible for getting rid of antiquated laws and devising new ones to enlarge individual freedom. Freedom includes freedom of choice and opportunity, as well as political freedom; and a government's responsibility includes the duty of constantly expanding freedom in all its forms.

MEANS

Democratic Socialism is more than a belief in individual equality and freedom. It is also the conscious, directed control of the social, political and economic machinery of a nation (and ultimately for the world) to obtain equality and freedom for all. Democratic Socialists have always argued that the unchecked

6 Harold Wilson, *The Relevance of British Socialism*. Weidenfeld and Nicolson, 1964. pp. 108–9.

workings of the forces of the market produce inequality and exploitation. Long and bitter experience has shown that vigorous government intervention in the form of control of the economy, public ownership of the basic industries, redistribution of wealth through taxation and social services, and egalitarian education, is necessary if society is to be changed in the direction of greater equality and freedom. Other men may talk but Socialists are prepared to use all the resources of legitimate action to ensure that these ideals become a practical reality.

Yet Democratic Socialists are realists. They are well aware that their whole programme cannot be carried out over-night. Resources are still scarce even in the richest of societies. Thus, at any given moment, there has to be choice between different parts of their programme. As Aneurin Bevan, the great British Labour Minister of Health, wrote, 'It [Democratic Socialism] accepts the obligation to choose among different kinds of social action and in so doing to bear the pains of rejecting what is not practicable or less desirable.' Above all, a Socialist government has to retain the support of the people.

Despite these limitations on how much can be achieved in a short period, Democratic Socialists seldom allow means to become divorced from ends. Their great ideals give meaning to the work of Socialist governments. Thus they are quite prepared to modify traditional policies once it has become clear that these no longer help to achieve their ideals. They accept, too, the verdict of the democratic electorate even if it goes against them because the right of free choice of government is part of the freedom for which they are fighting.

3 Control of the Economy: Planning and Public Ownership

The late 1940s saw the first real flowering of parliamentary Socialism. In most European countries, Socialist governments or left-wing coalitions with Socialist participation were swept to power.

War often brings social change with it. The 1939–45 war, like the 1914–18 war, opened up new opportunities for Socialists. In Britain, the Labour Party had a real share of power in Churchill's wartime coalition of 1940–45. It was the Labour Party's acceptance of office under Churchill which was the crucial factor in the formation of his government, and Labour Members of Parliament gave more wholehearted support to Churchill than those Conservatives who had been followers of Chamberlain. Labour Ministers, including Bevin, Morrison, Cripps, and above all Attlee, occupied key positions in Churchill's war cabinet, and were able to initiate the movement for social change which was to give them undisputed power in 1945.

Attlee said of the work of Churchill's coalition government, 'When one came to work out solutions they were often socialist ones, because one had to have organisation, and planning, and disregard private interests.' The progressive taxation of wartime Chancellors, the Beveridge Report of 1942 which was instigated by Arthur Greenwood as Minister in charge of reconstruction, and the acceptance of planning for full employment, all prepared the way for a Labour Government. The British people agreed with Attlee when he said during the

1945 election campaign, '... If in war, despite the diversions of most of our energies to making instruments of destruction, and despite the shortage of supply imposed by war conditions, we were able to provide food, clothing and employment for all our people, it is not impossible to do the same in peace, provided the government has the will and the power to act.' Impressed by the performance of Labour Ministers during the war, and rejecting the performance of Conservative governments before the war, the British electorate returned, for the first time, a majority Labour Government with an overwhelming mandate for change and reconstruction.

Most other Western European countries went Left.[1] The war had discredited the right-wing parties, and Socialists, Communists, and the religious parties played a prominent part in the resistance movements against Hitler. In Australasia, the New Zealand and Australian Labour parties gained credit and further office from their conduct of the war. The late 1940s in Western Europe and Australasia saw an attack on poverty, injustice and privilege that was qualitatively different from any before. In Britain the Labour administrations of 1945–51, so far the greatest reforming administration in Britain's history, began a transformation of the social and economic structure of the country. They established full employment; took the basic industries into public ownership; through redistributive taxation brought about greater equality of wealth; and introduced a really comprehensive system of social security. In Norway and Australia, Socialist governments brought full employment and social security to their countries. In Sweden and New Zealand the Social Democrat and Labour governments developed the work they had begun in the 1930s. In Holland, Denmark, Switzerland, Austria, Belgium, Italy and France, Socialist parties joined coalition governments, and in most of these countries were able to introduce a series of far-reaching reforms. In France, for example, both the French planning

1 In Eastern Europe, Socialists shared power with the Communists in the beginning but were soon pushed out of office by the Russians.

system and comprehensive social services owe their existence in the main to socialist initiatives.

Back-handed tributes to Socialist and left-wing achievement in the 1940s came from two very different sources. Stalin genuinely believed that the end of the war in Europe would bring with it a series of catastrophic slumps which would lead to a Communist takeover of Western Europe. Today the idea that Western Europe is facing desperate economic crisis has been tacitly dropped by Communist leaders. There are two reasons for Western Europe's dramatic recovery; first, the generous aid given by the United States to Western Europe, and second, the new direction taken by Socialist and left-wing governments from 1945 which ensured that American aid was wisely absorbed. On the Right, conservative leaders are now committed to most measures carried out during the creative period of the 1940s, including planning for full employment and economic expansion, and the creation of comprehensive social services.

Control of the Economy

It was impossible to begin the building of an egalitarian, socially just society without, first, ensuring that every man had a job. The right to work is a basic human right—as long ago as 1907 the British Labour Party had introduced a Right to Work Bill which sought statutory recognition of the right to a reasonable job for all who were able and willing to work; and without full employment it was impossible to establish and pay for an adequate system of social services. Just as full employment was a precondition of an egalitarian society, so the social services provide a built-in stabiliser against depression.

The series of booms and slumps, the socially unjust distribution of rewards, and above all the mass unemployment of the 1930s had finally established that the uncontrolled workings of the moment and the profit motive alone could never produce a stable, egalitarian society. The full powers of government had to be used if full employment was to be ensured. This implied use of all the fiscal weapons at the government's command, a new set of social priorities, and new planning techniques.

Planning for full employment was not enough. Governments had also to plan to increase the nation's wealth. For increased national wealth, if fairly shared, meant increased personal incomes and, therefore, an increase in individual opportunity. It was also impossible to improve the social services without an increase in national wealth. Socialists rejected the idea that the sum of numerous individual investment decisions could provide an adequate way to plan for economic growth. Only central planning could ensure a steady increase in national wealth. This chapter, therefore, analyses not only the innovations of Socialists in planning for full employment and their policies on public ownership but also the planning techniques they devised to ensure economic expansion.

Planning for Full Employment

The earliest example of the successful use of planning to secure full employment is that of the Swedish Social Democrat government of 1932–36. The government was formed at the worst period of the Great Depression. Business activity in Sweden was at a low level. There had been a sharp fall in capital investment, and the crash of the Kreuger business empire had nearly brought the Swedish banking system down with it. Production had dropped 34 per cent in the export industries and 13 per cent in the domestic industries. By January 1933 the monthly average of unemployed had risen from 10,000 in 1929 to 189,225.

The Social Democrat unemployment programme contained two new ideas. The first was a systematic use of government-financed public works to provide employment and stimulate the economy; the second was a deliberate effort to increase purchasing power, both by the use of deficit government financing and by the redistribution of income in the form of social services and subsidies to the industrial working classes and the farming community.

PUBLIC WORKS

Under a new Ministry of Social Affairs, headed by Gustav Moller, the entirely inadequate and ill-organised relief work introduced earlier in the century as a form of charity was converted into a dynamic public works programme. All state and municipal public works programmes planned for the future were begun immediately; subsidies were given for state works and buildings such as schools and hospitals, for railways, roads and harbour construction, and for improvements in forestry and agriculture. To increase purchasing power, men employed on public works were to get the full market wage rather than the pittance workers had received under the relief work system, which was 15 per cent below the minimum wage which an unskilled labourer could earn in the open market. The result of this new public works programme was that 34,545 men, or nearly half of the total reduction of 80,000 in the number of unemployed between October 1933 and October 1934, found work on public projects. But the public works programme had wider efforts— its projects stimulated activity in the construction industries, which, in its turn, had an expansionary effect on the whole economy. For the first time, public investment was used to provide the motor for the economy.

DEFICIT BUDGETING AND SOCIAL SECURITY

A crucial part of the Social Democrat government's unemployment policies was its deficit budgeting. For if the money needed to finance the public works programme had been raised by the then accepted method of taxation, the result would have been to neutralise the stimulus to the economy which the public works provided. So Ernst Wigforss, the Minister of Finance, deliberately unbalanced his budgets by resorting to loans to finance the public works programme.

The Social Democrat government also introduced new social security measures, not only to provide new weapons against poverty but also to increase the purchasing power of the poorer sections of the community. These measures had the effect of stimulating economic activity, thereby creating new employment. An extensive system of state-backed unemployment insurance was created; old age pensions were increased and special housing loans were given to large families. Money was found for these services by increased taxation on larger incomes and by higher inheritance taxes rather than by deficit budgeting. At the same time the purchasing power of the farming community, badly hit by the slump, was increased by guaranteed prices for agricultural goods, special grants were made for the rebuilding of farm buildings and for the improvement of rural housing, and agricultural credit was made easier.

The unemployment figures tell their own story. By October 1933, unemployment, which had reached 189,225, or about 25 per cent of the labour force in January 1933, was down to 165,000. In 1934 the average figure was down to 114,860, and by the middle of 1937 only 9,600 or about 2 per cent of the labour force were unemployed. Though, after 1934, Swedish exports benefited from the rearmament of the major European countries, in particular Germany, there is little doubt that it was the bold action of the Social Democrat government that was the decisive factor in getting rid of mass-unemployment.

LATER DEVELOPMENTS

Since then the weapons at a government's disposal for maintaining full employment and controlling the economy have multiplied. The budget and the control of government expenditure have been used by all Western European governments to secure full employment and to control the running of both public and private sectors of the economy. The budget is used to stimulate or restrict demand by cutting or increasing taxes and government expenditure. In most Western European countries, the government's share of total expenditure has been increased by the large public sectors created in the 1940s. Methods have also been developed not only of controlling the running of the economy, but also of influencing particular private firms and industries. Discriminating taxes or subsidies, legislative action such as restrictive practices or the location of industry, hire-purchase controls, and its power as a final buyer means that a government can if it wants influence particular sections of the economy.

These developments of the techniques first used by the Swedish Social Democrats have given governments the weapons not only to plan for full employment but also for long-term economic expansion (as is described in the last section of this chapter). The results of these new planning techniques, if considered from the full-employment point of view alone, are remarkable. In the 1950s most Western European countries had under 2·5 per cent unemployed. The substitution of a planned adjustment of demand for a rudderless free-enterprise system has 'ironed' out the erratic cycle of booms and slumps which produced such terrible mass unemployment.

Public Ownership

THE MIXED ECONOMY

Marx said, '. . . The theory of the Communists may be summed up in the single sentence: Abolition of private property' (*Manifesto of the Communist Party*, 1848). For Marx believed that the only way to transform the social system was by a complete change in property relationships. To Marx, private ownership of the means of production was wrong in itself, and any reform which did not abolish it altogether was inadequate.

Most early Socialist political leaders assumed with Marx that Socialism meant public ownership of *all* the means of production, distribution and exchange; and most of the first manifestoes or constitutions of Socialist parties (including the 1891 Erfurt programme of the German Social Democrats, the 1897 programme of the Swedish Social Democrats, and even to some extent the 1918 constitution of the British Labour

Party) called for public ownership of all property. Two factors modified Socialist views on public ownership. First and most important, Socialists, in power, have developed techniques of controlling the economy; also, in redistributive taxation and social services, they have found powerful weapons to correct social injustice. Thus it was not necessary either from the point of economic efficiency or of social justice to carry out a *universal* transformation from private to public ownership. Secondly, there was evidence that public ownership need not be specifically Socialist and, in fact, in the wrong hands could provide a very effective instrument of political tyranny. Even European conservative governments were forced, for a lack of any alternative, to nationalise some of the basic industries. In Germany, the nationalisation of the railways was very largely carried out by the arch-conservative Bismarck; in Sweden part of the forests, the railways, and the electricity power system were taken into public ownership long before the first Social Democrat government; in Britain it was a Conservative government which set up the British Broadcasting Corporation and the British Overseas Airways. A more sinister development was the use during the 1930s of public corporations by the Nazis in Germany and Austria, and by the Fascists in Italy, to further their own totalitarian power and to prepare for war. But the biggest blow of all to the idea that wholesale public ownership necessarily promotes Socialist aims was the example of Russia. The Russian Communists nationalised all the means of production, distribution and exchange, but the result under Stalin (as Khrushchev himself admitted at the 1956 Twentieth Party Congress in Moscow) was certainly not equality or freedom.

Today Democratic Socialists take a much more discriminating attitude towards public ownership. In the words of the 1951 Socialist International which met at Frankfurt, 'Socialist planning does not presuppose public ownership of all the means of production.' The German Social Democrats, in their Bad Godesburg programme of 1959 declared, 'Private ownership of the means of production can claim protection by society as long as it does not hinder the establishment of social justice.' The Swedish Social Democrats' 1960 manifesto stated, 'Social Democracy supports the demand for public ownership or public control of natural resources and enterprises, to the extent that it is necessary to safeguard important public interests'; and in the same year the British Labour Party reinterpreted Clause Four of the Party's constitution (which called for 'common ownership of the means of production, distribution and exchange') in these words: 'Recognising that both public and private enterprise have a place in the economy it believes that further extension of common ownership should be decided from time to time in light of these objectives (control of the economy and social justice), and according to circumstances with due regard for the views of the workers and consumers concerned.'

Socialists regard public ownership as a vital part of their policies. Public ownership of the natural monopolies or basic industries is essential for planning. But they accept the existence of a 'mixed economy' with both a public and private sector, and are prepared to argue the case for extensions of public ownership in a practical, undogmatic way

THE PATTERN OF PUBLIC OWNERSHIP

The reforms of the 1940s gave most Western European countries large public sectors. There are four European countries, Britain, Austria, France and Italy, whose productive public enterprises have a 25 per cent share in national gross fixed investment or more.

Publicly-owned basic industries form the biggest part of the public sector. Though all advanced industrialised countries in Western Europe, America and Australasia have some basic industries in public ownership, only the Socialist governments of the 1940s provided a coherent strategy for public acquisition of the basic industries. The British Labour administrations of 1945–51 took most basic industries into public ownership.

They nationalised railways, civil aviation, road haulage; electricity, coal and atomic energy; cable and wireless; and steel. Labour presented the case for public ownership on two levels: first, the general planning case against the natural monopolies being left in private hands; second, the reasons for public ownership special to each industry. In particular they stressed the second level of reasons. Successive independent commissions set up by non-Labour governments had recommended radical reorganisation of the coal industry (the 1919 Sankey Commission had gone so far as to recommend nationalisation); and bitter experience had shown that the coal owners blocked reorganisation, had very bad relations with the miners, and could not attract the necessary capital. Similarly, the McGowan Report on Electricity Distribution (1936) had called for far-reaching structural reforms, while the Heyworth Report on the gas industry (1945) had proposed outright nationalisation.

The characteristic of the British Labour nationalisation acts of 1945–51 was the creation of public ownership of a whole industry. The form of organisation favoured by the Labour Government was the public corporation. They could have followed the example of the British Post Office (and several of the Swedish nationalised industries) and put the nationalised industry directly under the control of a government department. But the case for the public corporation had been argued convincingly in 1933 by Herbert Morrison[2] in his book *Socialization of Transport*. The public corporation has the advantage of combining parliamentary control with some measure of independence for the board of the nationalised industry. The minister is responsible in Parliament for overall policy but not for day-to-day administration which is entirely the responsibility of the board. The minister, however, selects the board, who are chosen on grounds of ability. Though there have been

2 Morrison was later Lord President of the Council in charge of the nationalisation programme and chairman of the Labour Committee which produced the 1945 Labour manifesto *Let us face the Future*.

several cases of ministerial interference, particularly in civil aviation and transport under the Conservatives (and also of ministerial incompetence), on the whole the constitutional framework of public corporations for the state-owned monopolies has been a success.

In France, the left-wing coalition governments of 1945 and 1946, in which the Socialists played a predominant part, nationalised, in addition to the Bank of France and the four largest commercial banks, most of the basic industries—coal, gas, electricity, civil aviation, and the merchant navy. The railways had already been nationalised in 1936 by the Popular Front government. There was a general measure of agreement on the Socialist desire for public ownership of the basic industries because the desperate economic position of post-war France left no alternative. Private enterprise, already partly discredited for having collaborated with the Germans during the war, could not hope to provide either the reorganisation or the investment to put the country's badly damaged basic industries back on their feet.

Extensions of public ownership outside the basic industries came about less as a part of general Socialist strategy but more for reasons peculiar to the time and to the firm or industry concerned. In France, Germany, Italy and Austria the state found itself the owners of big industrial assets which had belonged to Nazis, Fascists, and collaborators. In France, for example, the Renault motor works, were taken into public ownership in 1945 because the owners had been working directly for the Germans. In Germany, the state took over from the Nazis the Volkswagen works. In Italy, the state found itself the inheritor of, among other enterprises, I.R.I. (the Institute of Industrial Reconstruction) which had been set up by Mussolini in Italy to rescue the commercial banks from the economic slump and held majority and minority holdings in a vast amount of small and large operating companies, including shipbuilding, chemicals and electricity supply. In Austria, the Socialist-Peoples' Party coalition took into public ownership all former German property in Austria, which included the two iron and steel firms Vöest and Alpine-Montan, the heavy engineering firm Schoeller-Bleckmann, and the oil industry, to prevent a direct Soviet take-over in accordance with the terms of the 1945 Potsdam Agreement under which all German property sited in the Soviet zone of occupation was to go to the Soviet Union by way of reparations.

NEW FORMS OF PUBLIC OWNERSHIP

Now that most of the basic industries of Western European countries are in public ownership (the last such case was the nationalisation of electric power by the Italian Centre-Left coalition in 1962), Socialists are turning to *competitive public ownership* as a way to bring efficiency into an important sector of the economy. The most quoted example is the striking success of Renault which, though entirely owned by the state, is in competition with other private French car-manufacturing firms. The director-general of Renault is appointed directly by the Minister of Industrial Production, with the advice of the Minister of Finance and Economic Affairs. He is assisted by a board, composed of seven members appointed by the Minister of Industrial Production, six by the trade unions, and two representatives of the consumer. The director-general is given a free hand on prices, profits, and development, including the raising of capital.

Socialists also are interested in the possibilities of the *mixed enterprise*, for two reasons: first, to ensure that where a government subsidises private firms there should be a government share in the profits and control; secondly, to create new industries or new employment that private enterprise does not have the capital or the incentive to carry out alone. Harold Wilson wrote, '. . . Where an undertaking's profits are wholly or mainly dependent on state orders, as in the parts of our aircraft industry, or the pharmaceutical industry, whose profits at the expense of the National Health Service are a public scandal, we reserve the right to share in those profits by a share in the equity.'[3] In Israel, which is a developing country, the mixed firm has been used not so much to protect the government's interests but to initiate new enterprise. For example, Mekorot, the Israeli Water Development Corporation, which controls large-scale irrigation projects and the installation of water services, is financed and controlled by a partnership between the government, the Jewish Agency (the voluntary body concerned with immigration) and the Histadruth (the trade union organisation).

Some Socialists advocate a new type of public ownership with the aim, not of control, but of providing more investment capital for growth and of redistributing wealth to the benefit of the community.[4] For example, the British Labour Party has called for the profitable investment of their proposed National Pensions Fund in equity shares. The result would be to enable the community as a whole to share the benefits of prosperity.

Socialists also encourage the growth of other forms of 'social' or 'non-private' ownership, such as municipal and co-operative enterprises. They support these forms of 'social' enterprise because they supply services that would otherwise be entirely neglected. Without municipal enterprise in housing the need for cheap rented accommodation will be left almost entirely unfilled. Social enterprise, because it is non-private, also helps the redistribution of wealth.

The aim of Democratic Socialism is a flexible pattern of ownership, with public ownership of basic industries, selective nationalisation, mixed ownership, and municipal, co-operative, trade union and socially responsible private ownership as well. Socialists believe that public ownership, without having the unique significance ascribed to it by Communists and Marxists, should play an important role in promoting economic expansion, and redistributing national wealth.

3 In *The Relevance of British Socialism.* p. 39.
4 For a Swedish view see *Economic Expansion and Structural Change: A Trade Union Manifesto.* Allen and Unwin, 1963. pp. 156–66.

Planning for Economic Expansion

Common to all planning for economic expansion is the planning of production and investment. But the type of planning favoured by democratic countries is different in kind from communist planning. Russian planning, introduced in 1928 by Stalin, is still planning by government order rather than by mutual agreement between manufacturers, farmers, workers and government on the democratic pattern. Democratic planning also has to take consumer choice into account. Communist planning has been characterised (though recent Polish plans have shown a new respect for consumer choice) by the concentration on the needs of heavy industry at the expense of the consumer. There may have been little alternative during the period of Russian industrialisation; but the dead hand of Russian planning now prevents the Russian consumer from getting the goods to which he should be entitled. This section on planning for economic expansion describes the French planning system. Though it is by no means faultless, it is the earliest and still one of the most highly developed democratic planning systems.

AIMS AND ACHIEVEMENTS

Inspired by Socialists, and set up in January 1946 by a coalition government in which the Socialists played a leading part, the French plan now has the backing of all sections of the French nation. French planning was pioneered by the French Socialist party and the Conféderation Général du Travail during the 1930s. The destruction caused by the 1939–45 war converted most Frenchmen to the need for planning. The 'Resistance Charter', drawn up in March 1944 by the main French resistance movements, mostly with Socialist or left-wing sympathies, called for 'the intensification of national production along lines determined by the state after consultation with the representatives of all elements of production'. The election of a left-wing majority in October 1945 forced

General de Gaulle, who was head of the provisional government, to set up planning machinery. The decree of January 1946 established the Commissariat Général du Plan and a Commissaire Général (the great European Jean Monnet) was appointed. The decree of January 1946 stated that the purpose of the plan was 'to increase output in metropolitan France and the overseas territories and their trade with the rest of the world, more especially in those products in which their position is most favourable; to raise the productivity of labour to the level of those countries where it is highest; to ensure full employment of the labour force; to raise the standard of living of the population and to improve housing conditions and the circumstances of community life.'

French planning has been carried forward by a series of plans each of approximately four-year duration. The First Plan (1947–52) covered only the basic sectors of the economy. The emphasis, after the war destruction, was on the reconstruction of the strategic industries on which the growth of the rest of the economy was based. The planners' task was made much easier by the fact that, of the six basic industries, coal mines, electricity and transport had been taken into public ownership. The Second Plan (1954 57) was more ambitious. The scope of the plan was widened to include manufacturing industries, every aspect of agriculture, housing, education and health. Improvements in national accounting techniques enabled the second plan to forecast development not merely sector by sector but for the economy as a whole. The Third Plan (1958–61) covered every sector of the economy except for defence (including regional development). The existence of an input-output table enabled the planners to assign to the various branches of private industry more accurate targets for production and investment. It is with the Third Plan that democratic planning first appears in a reasonably developed form. In the Fourth Plan (1961–65) the planners have been able to sketch out in some detail alternative paths that the economy could follow over the period. The Fourth Plan also contains an attempt to 'formulate a growth path for the French economy which postulates not only a certain rate of growth but a certain pattern of growth. Thus, the growth of private consumption is to be held back to allow a greater effect in the field of social investment.'[5]

Though it is impossible to calculate exactly how much French economic expansion is attributable to planning, growth has been vigorous since planning was introduced. Since 1950, the growth rate of the French economy (the most sluggish in Europe between the two world wars) has been one of the fastest in Europe, averaging about 4 per cent a year—nearly double that of Britain and the United States. National production increased 70 per cent between 1949 and 1961.

THE MACHINERY OF PLANNING

The staff of the Commissariat Général du Plan now numbers only 150, and is divided into sections each responsible for the principal sectors of the economy. The Commissariat Général du Plan, together with the Ministry of Finance, works out preliminary forecasts a year before the plan is put into operation.[6] On the basis of these forecasts the government lays down the principle objectives of the plan. These forecasts are then put before the Modernisation Commissions, of which there is one for each sector. The Modernisation Commissions, whose personnel are appointed by the Prime Minister, represent the sectional interests involved, and are composed of civil servants, representatives of the employers, industrial and agricultural unions, and independent experts. Their job is to elaborate the preliminary forecasts for the sector concerned. Their work done, the Commissariat Général then combines the conclusions of the Commissions into one general report by which the French economy must be guided for the next four years.

5 See 'French planning: Some lessons for Britain', *Political and Economic Planning*, Sept. 1963.
6 For further details see Pierre Bauchet's book, *Economic Planning: The French Experience*. Heinemann, 1964.

Though the creation of the plan is a collective effort, the government does, in fact, have weapons at its disposal to ensure that the plan is carried out. A key role is played by the public sector. The fact that the nationalised industries' share of the total fixed capital formation is about 25 per cent, and that together with the government they control over 30 per cent of total national expenditure and over 50 per cent of total national investment, means that the government is not only able to plan production and investment in the public sector but also influence the production and investment plans of the private sector. The French nationalised industries, like the nationalised industries in Austria and Italy, are the spearhead of economic expansion. The First Plan channelled investment into the nationalised industries, which created a sound basis for the expansion of the rest of the economy. The nationalised industries have been in the van of technological advance—for example, the production of the Caravelle, the electrification of the railways, and the Renault motor cars; and, through their orders placed in the private sector of the economy, have been used as one of the key weapons of the French planning system.

The government has other weapons at its disposal. These include direct restraints such as building permits, control over development in the Paris district and petrol refinery permits. But usually the government prefers to act indirectly; negatively through control of credit and new bond issues; positively through tax reliefs, investment bonuses and subsidies.

DEFECTS

The defects of French planning spring from the fact that it has mostly been carried out by non-Socialist governments. There are three main weaknesses. First, there has been a timidity about using all the machinery to enforce planning targets and decisions. In particular the government has shrunk from creating (or threatening to create) publicly owned corporations to increase production in strategic industries or in particular regions of France. Secondly, there has been far too little parliamentary control of the plan. The Modernisation Commissions and the Economic and Social Council (a non-elective body to which the plans are referred at an early stage) ensure group representation. But only the Second and Fourth Plans were put before parliament—though the basic aims of future Plans will be submitted to parliament.

The most important defect of French planning, however, is the degree to which organised labour has been excluded from the plans. The trade unions are under-represented on the Modernisation Commissions and there is no attempt at any form of incomes policy (discussed in Chapter 7). With the existence of a large private capital market, growth in the economy, without a redistribution of profits, is bound to increase the wealth of a small section of the population; and it is difficult to demand sacrifices from the wage earners merely to add to other people's wealth. Under de Gaulle, the question of the distribution of wealth has not been seriously tackled. French planning has become planning without social justice and very often without firmness and direction. A Socialist planning system would require more systematic and intelligent use of the weapons at the government's disposal—and a more developed sense of social priorities.

4 Towards Equality: The Social Services and Redistributive Taxation

Democratic Socialists have always given high priority to government social services because they believe that, as part of the battle for social equality and justice, it should be a collective responsibility to ensure a fair share of the basic necessities of life for all citizens. This implies that everyone should have the right to a pension, the proper medical attention, to a decent home and a good education. Socialist governments pioneered many of the advances in social welfare; and most of the new thinking on welfare comes from Socialists (for example, the Swedish Social Democrats and the British Labour Party). Perhaps the greatest tribute to Socialist achievement in this field is that most governments of the 'affluent' countries, of whatever political persuasion, now support, more or less sincerely, the idea of social welfare.

THE FINANCING OF THE SOCIAL SERVICES
Some European countries now spend nearly 20 per cent of their gross national product on social services (including housing and education). The financing of these services depends on the maintenance of full employment and economic expansion. Yet the social services are, themselves, a way of ensuring both full employment and economic expansion. The provision of social services increases the purchasing power of the lower-income groups and thus acts as a built-in stabiliser. The social services have also made a contribution to economic growth. 'The main growth contribution of these social transfers has been to promote confidence amongst the population generally.

... This has encouraged European entrepreneurs to feel that major depressions are no longer on the cards and that recessions will be brief and modest.'[1] Because they support the principle of social justice, Socialist governments have given priority to the financing of social services (and, indeed, other public services such as defence) by progressive taxation rather than by regressive flat-rate levies. Progressive taxation ensures that the better-off sections of the community pay proportionately more than the poorer sections of the community, while flat-rate levies fall most heavily on the poorer sections of the community, so that social services are financed almost entirely from the pockets of working-classes.

SOCIAL SECURITY BENEFITS

By 1950, many Western European countries had introduced systems of basic social security. The New Zealand Labour government's Social Security Act of 1938 had been followed, among others, by the British Labour government's National Insurance Act of 1946, the French Coalition government's Social Security Legislation of 1946, and the Swedish Social Democrat government's National Pension Act of 1946 and General Health Insurance Act of 1947. The common principle behind these social security acts was that they were designed to secure a basic minimum standard of living for all in times of unemployment, ill-health, and old age, and for those with large families.

The social security schemes played an important part in reducing primary poverty (poverty due directly to insufficient earnings). The British sociologist, B. Seebohm Rowntree,[2] carried out two investigations into the incidence of poverty in York, one in 1936, the other in 1950. He found that, whereas in 1936, 31 per cent of the working class were living below the

1 Angus Maddison, *Economic Growth in the West*. Allen and Unwin, 1964.
2 Seebohm Rowntree and G. R. Lavers, *Poverty and the Welfare State*. Longmans, 1951.

poverty line, in 1950 the percentage had fallen to 3 per cent. Full employment and vertical redistribution of income resulted in a general rise in the working-class standards, and thus, helped to reduce the incidence of poverty. But Labour's social security schemes ensured that the groups most susceptible to poverty—the old, the sick, and large families—shared in the rising standard of living. Seebohm Rowntree and Lavers calculated that had welfare legislation remained unchanged during the intervening years, the percentage of working-class families in poverty would have been, not 3 per cent, but 22 per cent.

These social security schemes were designed to secure a minimum standard of living or subsistence security. Contributions and benefits were usually flat-rate rather than wage-related; and the British scheme did not have any mechanism whereby social security benefits could keep pace with the rise in the cost of living. A major departure in social security was the Swedish National Pensions Act of 1960, which was introduced by the Social Democrat government headed by Tage Erlander, Prime Minister since 1946, and passed by one vote in the Swedish Lower House after a national referendum. The idea underlying a big increase in pensions in Sweden was that the standard of living enjoyed in old age should correspond to the standard of living enjoyed during working life—in 1964 the highest standard of living in Europe. By the Act of 1960 the original 1946 flat-rate pension was supplemented by a further pension financed exclusively by employers' contributions based on a percentage of each individual employee's income. The total retirement pension amounts to two-thirds of the average income during the last fifteen years before retirement; and both pensions are tied to the cost of living. State pensions in Sweden are now equal to the best private pension, so that all can now enjoy an equally secure old age.

The Labour government has begun a comprehensive reform of the British social security system. Based on ideas put forward when Labour was in opposition, this reform is designed to bring not only old age pensions but also sickness and unemployment benefits up to the standard of the Swedish pensions scheme. Labour is introducing an income-related superannuation scheme which guarantees about half-pay on retirement; and an income-related sickness and unemployment benefit which guarantees half-pay or more during the first year's absence from work. Contributions will be income-related and shared between employer and employee, while the remainder of the money needed to finance Labour's reforms will come from general taxation. The income-related principle will ensure both that contributions are based on ability to pay and that benefits are related not to subsistence but to rising income levels.

HEALTH SERVICE

One of the greatest achievements of the British Labour administration of 1945–51 was the introduction in 1948 of a National Health Service which was free to the user (though paid for by taxation), universal in scope and comprehensive in character. Ten years earlier Michael Savage's Labour government had introduced a Health Service in New Zealand. Though this service was designed to give 'every member of the community full and adequate hospital, sanatoria, medical, pharmaceutical, maternity and other health services', it was less comprehensive than the British Health Service.

Aneurin Bevan, Labour Minister of Health, who introduced the British Health Service, said that 'the essence of the satisfactory health service is that the rich and the poor are treated alike, that poverty is not a disability and wealth is not an advantage.' Though before 1948, under the system of National Insurance introduced by the Liberal Chancellor of the Exchequer Lloyd George, in 1911, there had been some form of aid to those who were ill, medical services for the working- and middle-classes alike were quite inadequate—and the chronic sick who needed the most comprehensive medical services were given the least adequate coverage. Illness was not only a physical but also a financial scourge. The National Health Service gave every individual the right of free access to the most expensive and comprehensive treatment, including specialist, surgical, dental and ophthalmic services; it rationalised the chaotic hospital system by bringing all hospitals under public ownership; and introduced a tripartite system of general medical services, hospitals, and local health authorities.

The National Health Service was almost immediately a triumphant success. Within a year of its introduction, although the service was voluntary, 95 per cent of the eligible population were covered by it. Fourteen years later a Gallup Poll survey showed that 90 per cent of the British public were in favour of the Health Service, while a survey by Political and Economic Planning found that the Health Service was the most widely used and appreciated of all the social services. The Labour government has embarked on a further series of badly needed reforms, including better facilities for general practitioners, and the building of more hospitals. But, though the Health Service is not yet perfect, there is no denying that it has brought about a revolution in health standards and removed the fear of crippling medical bills from every household.

HOUSING

Socialists believe that the provision of adequate housing for all sections of the community cannot be left to the forces of the market. If housing was left entirely to private enterprise, there would be little building to meet the working population's needs. For private builders only find it profitable to meet the middle-class demand. In Britain, for example, it was calculated that two-thirds of households cannot afford the economic rent of a new house, and seven-eighths cannot afford to buy a new house out of income[3] and the same proportions probably hold good for most of the developed countries of the

3 L. Needleman, 'A Long Term View of Housing', *National Institute Economic Review*, November 1961.

world. That is why Socialist governments and local authorities in Scandinavia, Britain, Austria, Germany, and Australasia have pioneered the idea of public housing—an idea which is now followed by most governments and local authorities in the developed countries.

Sweden is, perhaps, the country with the most developed public housing policy. There, government and local authorities accept responsibility for seeing everyone has a home. The local authorities are bound by law to provide adequate housing for all sections of the community. To provide cheap housing, the government grants the local authorities loans for building at advantageous terms; and the government imposes a rent control on most types of housing. Many local authorities help to keep down construction costs by employing non-profit making construction firms, initiated by and under the control of the local authorities; a third of all dwellings are now built by these non-profit making firms. Just under a third of all dwellings are built by co-operative organisations, including the Tenants Savings and Loan Association and the building trade unions, which are supported by government loans. In addition to these general government subsidies, particular sections of the community receive special subsidies. Large families and families with limited incomes get rent allowances; pensioners get rent allowances to enable the local authorities to provide 'pensioners' flats in local authority flats; and house owners (particularly in rural areas) receive loans on favourable terms to cover the cost of improvements.

The results of the Swedish housing policy can be summed up by the following sets of figures. In 1945, 21 per cent of Swedish households were considered overcrowded (more than two persons to a room). In 1962 it was down to 10 per cent. More than one-fifth of all houses have been built since 1945. In 1939, the average rent for a new Swedish flat (of two rooms and a kitchen) was about 35 per cent of an average industrial wage. Partly as a result of government housing subsidies and rent control, the rent proportion had fallen to 17 per cent in 1955.

In Britain, governments face particularly difficult housing problems: Britain is the third most densely populated country in the world and has a large stock of obsolete houses. But a combination of inadequate planning machinery, inefficient building methods, a shift of government investment away from housing, and high land prices, held back the building of houses during the 1950s and 1960s. On return to office in 1964, the Labour government prepared a fresh approach. Its main elements were an increased share of investment for public housing, more efficient building methods, special provisions for prospective owner occupiers and the setting up of a Land Commission. The task of the Land Commission was to speed up the procedure for bringing land onto the market, to provide planned development, and to ensure that the community shared in increased land values.

EDUCATION

Democratic Socialists believe that every man is entitled to equal educational opportunities, regardless of birth, wealth, colour, creed or ability. Without education, the individual cannot develop his potentialities to the full and so is deprived of effective freedom of choice in his job and in his leisure. Without education, the community cannot provide each new generation with the skills necessary for development of society and technological change. If restricted access to educational opportunities creates class-ridden societies, equal opportunity is one of the most important prerequisites of a classless society. For all these reasons, Socialist governments have given special priority to the development of a free state system of education which gives equal opportunity to all.

Socialists share with Canadian and American politicians and educationalists the credit for developing a system of education which offers (at least in theory) equal opportunity. But though the United States has a fully fledged comprehensive system and gives 38 per cent of the young people between eighteen and twenty-one some kind of higher education (the

highest for any country), its educational system is still, in spite
of action by the United States government, marred by the
fact that as in so many other aspects of American life, Negro
children have for the most part worse opportunities than white
children. In Sweden, however, the educational system offers
real equality of opportunity up to university level. The Swedish
system is based on free comprehensive schooling for all to
the age of sixteen. Schooling begins at seven, and is divided up
into three-year stages—seven to ten, ten to thirteen, thirteen
to sixteen. The purpose of comprehensive schools is to ensure
that all children, regardless of differences of ability, should
have access to full primary and secondary education. Though
differences of ability and skills are respected, comprehensive
schools ensure that these differences in ability are reflected by
differences in kind of education not in quality. Surveys by
Swedish sociologists have shown that able children work, if
anything, better in comprehensive schools than separate
schools, while less able children make spectacular progress in
the stimulating atmosphere of the comprehensive school.
Comprehensive education also ensures that differences in
ability do not lead to social distinctions. The sons and daugh-
ters of Prime Ministers and bus conductors go to the same
kind of school.

Under the Conservatives, British education, in spite of pioneering in the development of the comprehensive school by
the Labour-controlled London County Council, was based on
division and class distinction. At the age of eleven, children at
state primary schools were channelled, on the basis mainly of
intelligence tests, into different types of secondary schools—
the grammar school for the bright child, the secondary modern
for the less bright. The main criticism of the eleven plus exam
(as it was called) was that it favoured the middle-class child
because it measured not just intelligence but also social and
educational background. It also led to waste of resources.
There was another even less justified distinction in the British
primary and secondary school system. Middle-class parents

were able to buy their children entry to private, fee-paying schools which had smaller classes and much greater social prestige than the free state schools. It is a curious fact that, under the Conservatives, this source of class distinction was supported by government tax concessions (which amounted to over a quarter of total private school fees). The apex of British education was a system of higher education in which there were places for only three out of every five students qualified.

It was no wonder that, under the Conservatives, Britain was largely run by an *élite* based on money and was, despite the work of the Labour administrations of 1945–51, a country riven by class differences. The Labour government is attempting to change the class structure of British society by radical educational reforms. These include the abolition of the eleven plus and the reconstruction of secondary education on comprehensive lines, the integration of private secondary education into the public system, and the general expansion of educational services.

REDISTRIBUTIVE TAXATION

The main weapon of government in the equalising of wealth and the promotion of social justice is progressive direct taxation and its redistribution in the form of social services.

The basic principle of progressive taxation is a larger proportionate contribution from those with a larger capacity to pay. Direct taxation can take many forms: it can be a tax on income; it can be a tax on property at death or a tax on the exchange of capital during lifetime; it can be a small annual wealth tax on all property above a certain level; or a tax on capital gains.

As a redistributive weapon, progressive direct taxation is far superior to indirect taxation. The latter, usually levied on consumer goods, falls proportionately most heavily on the poorer classes because they spend a higher proportion of their income; it is also much less easy to adjust it to individual cases. The lower level of direct taxation in Italy and France than in

Britain or Sweden is one of the main reasons for the visibly greater economic inequality in Italy and France; and in the Soviet Union, where there is a wide gap between the living standards of the higher and lower income groups, 92 per cent of government revenue comes from a turnover or indirect tax on consumer goods and deductions from the profits of state enterprises; and there is an extremely low and unprogressive rate of income tax on earned income. Progressive direct taxation is also a much quicker way of redistributing wealth than the spread of public ownership. This is because the acquisition of an industry involves compensation to the shareholders. For example, when the British Labour government of 1945–51 nationalised coal mines, it paid full compensation based on the asset values of the shares to shareholders. Progressive direct taxation, however, in the words of the British Socialist, Douglas Jay, can strike 'at once at all profits whatever, and all forms of unearned income, such as rent and interest, and not just the "industry", at a time'.[4]

REDISTRIBUTION IN BRITAIN BETWEEN 1940 AND 1951

Five years of Coalition government, followed by six years of Labour government, brought with it a considerable change in the redistribution of wealth in Britain. In 1938 the share of wages in total disposable private income was 37 per cent (or about the same as it was in 1900) while the remaining 63 per cent went to the far smaller numbers living on salaries, rents, interests or profits. Inequality in the holding of property was even worse. In 1936, one per cent of the population over twenty-five owned over half the total property in private hands, 5 per cent owned 75–80 per cent, while three-quarters of the population owned only 5 per cent between them.[5]

Successive Chancellors of the Exchequer used progressive income tax as a way of redistributing income. As compared

4 Douglas Jay, *Socialism in the New Society*. Longmans, 1962. p. 181.
5 H. Campion, *Public and Private Property in Great Britain*. Oxford University Press, 1939. pp. 109–10.

with 1938, direct taxation in 1949 had risen from 9 per cent
to 18 per cent as a proportion of national income and from
35 per cent to 67 per cent as a proportion of total taxation.[6]
Secondly, direct taxation became more progressive. Comparing
1950 with 1938, a single man whose income was wholly
earned paid only £28 more in tax on an income of £500; £98
more on £1,000, and £2,280 more on £10,000, reducing his
net income from £5,867 to £3,587.[7] In addition, heavier
corporate taxation reduced the net profits available to companies for distribution, and so restrained rises both in dividend
disbursements and share prices. The result of the Coalition and
Labour governments' measures was that the wage earners'
share of total disposable real income rose by 10 per cent,
while the property owners' fell by 10 per cent—a transfer of
10 per cent of total disposable income from property owners
to the wage earners.

The distribution of property was not, however, significantly
altered by the Coalition and Labour governments. Though the
first two Labour Chancellors after the war, Hugh Dalton and
Sir Stafford Cripps, stiffened death duties on property (80 per
cent on millionaire estates), these taxes naturally worked
slowly. After 1951 Conservative governments made death
duties less effective by allowing property owners to escape
duty if they disposed of their capital five years before death.
In addition, during the 1950s, property owners benefited
almost exclusively from vast capital gains on equity shares.
Capital gains are an inevitable by-product of economic prosperity and growth; and it is manifestly unjust that an unfair
share of the fruits of growth (a national effort) should go un-
taxed to the already wealthy few. Today less than 2 per cent
of adult persons in Britain own 50 per cent of total personal
capital; 10 per cent of persons own nearly 80 per cent; while
75 per cent own less than 9 per cent. To prevent further

6 I. M. D. Little, *Fiscal Policy in The British Economy 1945–51*. Oxford
University Press, 1952.
7 C. A. R. Crosland, *The Future of Socialism*. Cape, 1956. p. 50.

increases in inequality resulting from capital gains, the British Labour government brought in a capital gains tax in 1965. In Sweden and Norway Socialist governments have attempted to iron out inequalities in property by the introduction of an annual wealth tax of between 0·25 per cent and 1·75 per cent on property above a certain exemption limit.

13775

5 Democratic Government

DEMOCRATIC SOCIALISM AND DEMOCRACY
Democratic institutions are the political expression of the Democratic Socialist principles of freedom and equality. Eduard Bernstein said in 1906: 'Democracy is at the same time means and end. It is the means of the struggle for Socialism and it is the form Socialism will take once it has been realised.' Only through democratic institutions can the basic political freedoms—freedom of speech, freedom of association and free choice of government—be preserved. Only within a democratic framework can freedom and equality find their fullest expression.

Democratic Socialists argue that, in Western democracies, revolution—in the Marxist-Leninist sense of unconstitutional and violent change—is both unnecessary and a debasement of fundamental human rights. There may well be times when revolution is the only course open to an oppressed people. But, when there is an opportunity of redressing wrongs democratically, then revolution is a costly, unnecessary aberration. Stalin, himself, admitted this in 1945 when he told Yugoslav Communist leaders, 'Today Socialism is possible even under the English monarchy. Revolution is no longer necessary everywhere.'[1] In a democracy, revolution is not only unnecessary, it is morally wrong. If it is possible to change a government in a democratic way, then the revolutionaries, by overturning a democratically elected government, are deliberately flouting the wishes of the majority of the people and, therefore, diminishing political freedom. It is an often quoted paradox that, to

1 *See* Milovan Djilas, *Conversations with Stalin*. Hart-Davis, 1962. p. 104.

defend political freedom, a democratic government may be forced to limit the freedom of revolutionary, non-democratic parties.

Democracy, in any case, has clear practical advantages over other forms of government. First, democratic government has the priceless advantage of securing the possibility of a regular change of political power without bloodshed. Secondly, democratic government, because it is responsible to public opinion, avoids monumental and tragic blunders on the scale of Stalin's agricultural collectivisation schemes or hideous crimes like Hitler's extermination of the Jews. Precisely because there is no real provision for criticism and no clear way that public opinion can express itself in non-democratic régimes, their leaders are liable to these colossal excesses and mistakes. Thirdly, democratic government, because it represents the people, can, as the examples of Britain under Churchill and Attlee, Sweden under Hansson and the United States under Roosevelt illustrate, provide strong leadership backed by national unity of a kind that totalitarian leaders can never hope to emulate.

Socialists have been among the staunchest defenders of democracy. It is true that the first democratic institutions in Britain, France and Germany were created by liberals and enlightened conservatives but always under pressure from the emerging labour movements and with the workers' vote in mind. It should not be forgotten that it was the German Social Democrats and the Austrian Socialists who brought responsible democratic government to their respective countries; while in Sweden it was a Liberal-Social Democrat coalition which first introduced universal suffrage. In 1898 the French Socialists played a prominent part in defending French parliamentary institutions against the pretensions of the army in the Dreyfus affair; and the German and Austrian Socialists were Hitler's chief opponents and among his chief victims. The Labour Party joined Churchill's coalition in 1940 to defend democracy against the two dictators, Hitler and Mussolini.

The Socialist reforms of the 1940s gave democracy a new strength. Between the wars the characteristic of democracy was its instability. In 1922 Mussolini overthrew the democratic Italian government and ruled Italy as a dictator for twenty-one years. In 1933 Hitler seized power, and ruled as dictator until defeated by the Allies in 1945. Democracy in Austria led to virtual civil war, a period of dictatorship, and the occupation by Hitler. In France and Britain, there were extremist movements and a deep ground-swell of unrest. The main reason for this instability was the existence of mass unemployment and an unfair division of wealth between different sections of the community. The Socialist reforms of the 1940s, which have now been accepted by nearly all democratic governments, by establishing full employment, a system of social services, and a fairer distribution of wealth, have given a new stability to democratic institutions.[2] It is revealing that those countries in Europe which are stable democracies had or have had a Socialist government.

THE ESSENTIALS OF DEMOCRACY

Three principles are essential to a democratic system: limitations on the power of the government in order to provide safeguards for individuals and minority groups; effective popular representation; and the constitutional and peaceful change of power.

If the rights of individuals are to be respected, there must be limitations on the power of government. In 1898 Bernstein wrote, 'The idea of democracy includes, in the conception of the present day, a notion of justice and equality of rights for all members of the community . . . in that principle, the rule of the majority . . . finds its limits.' In other words, democracy means a respect for the freedom and equality of the individual

2 S. M. Lipset in his *Political Man*, Mercury Books, 1963, pp. 45–76, establishes a clear correlation between, on the one hand, fair distribution of wealth, full employment, and social services, including education; and on the other hand, stable democracy.

whether he belongs to a majority or a minority. The mark of a democracy is its tolerance of dissent. In practice, this means that governments must abide by the rules of law. The rules of law limit the power of the government and define the basic rights of the citizen such as freedom from arbitrary arrest; the right to have one's case reviewed publicly before a judge within a limited period of time after arrest; the freedom of speech; the right to vote; and the right of association. In order that these rights should be observed, it is essential to have an independent judiciary.

Modern democracy, because nations are large and populations dispersed, is representative democracy rather than direct rule by the people on the Athenian model. Fully effective representation implies free elections with a genuine choice of candidates; an elected and fully representative assembly with powers strong enough to give the people a say in government; and the freedom to oppose and criticise, including the freedom of the press and the mass media.

The constitutional and peaceful change of power implies both the presence of legal and organised opposition, and the acceptance by all of the results of elections and other constitutional changes in power.

SYSTEMS OF DEMOCRATIC GOVERNMENT

Socialist parties have held power under different systems of democratic government. But though there are many different types of democratic systems, two examples stand out: the Parliamentary system and the Presidential system. In the Parliamentary system the executive takes its power from an elected parliament; in the Presidential system, the executive and the legislative are elected separately.

The most famous parliamentary system is the British. The British Cabinet (with the Prime Minister as by far its most powerful member) is one of the strongest executives in the democratic world. It provides an excellent instrument for a reforming government with a parliamentary majority which wants to get a great deal of business done in a short time, like the Labour administrations of the 1940s and 1960s. Even so, the British Parliament, in spite of its weaknesses (in particular that it has little real control over government expenditure or complicated policy questions such as defence), does provide an excellent forum for the opposition—as the use of Parliament by the Conservative opposition from 1947 to 1951 and the Labour opposition from 1961 to 1964 shows.

The Swedish parliamentary system is characterised by the special powers that are entrusted to parliament. Though a reforming government with a parliamentary majority, as in the case of the Social Democrats, can get its legislation through parliament, the powers of the Swedish executive are not so great as those of the British Prime Minister and his Cabinet. This is because of the control that the committees of parliament, which meet privately without the minister concerned, exert over government legislation; and because of the civil and military procurators appointed by parliament who keep the whole work of the executive under review.

The best-known example of the Presidential type of democratic government is that of the United States. The American Presidential system was designed to combine executive power and checks on executive power in a way that would be suitable to a vast country with many different minority groups. The President is not only elected separately but is also physically separated from the legislature. He has great sources of power. He controls the administration; is commander in chief of the armed forces and directs foreign policy; can appeal through press and television to the people; is leader of his party; and has a four, possibly eight, year term of office. But in spite of these powers he often has great difficulty in getting his legislation through the legislature. Congress may well be controlled, as it was in 1956, by a different party to that of the President. Congress also has a powerful committee system which decides the fate of the President's legislation. An American President, Woodrow Wilson, called the American system 'a government by the chairmen of the standing committees of Congress'. The system of having the Senior Representative or Senator as Chairman has, up until now, reinforced the position of the conservative Southern Democrats. In addition the electoral boundaries overweight the rural areas. For all these reasons the power of the American President, though formidable, is less impressive than it appears on paper.

Although the French Presidential system was created by de Gaulle for himself, it has, in fact, been accepted by the opposition parties who contested the 1965 Presidential elections. The constitution of the Fifth Republic is designed to give de Gaulle the executive power and to limit the power of the National Assembly which was the dominant feature of the Third and Fourth Republics. The sessions of the National Assembly are limited in time and scope; and the budget can in the final analysis be passed over its head. The President, who is elected by universal suffrage, can dissolve the National Assembly and take full emergency powers if necessary. In addition the executive controls radio and television, though not the press. Under de Gaulle, most of the fundamental liberties have been preserved, but there has been a dramatic increase in the power of the executive.

Both the American and French Presidents combine the political and ceremonial aspects of office in their person. De Gaulle performs the function not only of a British Prime Minister but also of a British hereditary monarch. As the existence of hereditary but constitutional monarchs in ten out of the twelve most stable European and English-speaking democracies shows, the ceremonial function is an important one. A President who combines both ceremonial and political functions can prove a very effective focus for national unity in a transition period, particularly in reconciling traditional elements to change.

There are many other differences in democratic practice. In the West, Socialist governments have held power under a variety of electoral systems. Good democrats—including

Democratic Socialists—are still arguing about the respective merits of election by majority vote and election by proportional representation; about direct or indirect methods of voting; about whether large or small, one-member or many-member electoral districts are best. They argue, too, about the intervals between elections, and whether, as in Sweden, it is fairer to have a fixed date for an election or, as in Britain, to leave the time, within limits, to be decided by the government. There may be two chambers (as in Britain, Sweden, or the United States) or there may be one (as in New Zealand). There are different legal systems. In the United States, for example, the judiciary (the Supreme Court) has the power to judge whether laws passed by Congress are legal. In Britain, however, Parliament alone is sovereign; the judiciary can only interpret the laws.

In this profusion of democratic practice, Democratic Socialists are not dogmatic; but they believe that there must be some form of effective popular representation, the possibility of constitutional and peaceful changes of power, and limitations on the power of the government.

DEMOCRATIC SOCIALIST PARTIES AND THE PARTY SYSTEM

The modern mass political party was the creation of Socialists. Political organisation was far more important to the working-class parties than to the parties of the Right, because the working-classes did not have the resources to compete electorally with middle-class parties, which were supported by big business. In nearly all democratic countries, the first highly organised mass party was Socialist. In Germany, the Christian Democrat Union (though it receives heavy subsidies from big business) has still not reached the degree of organisation which is the characteristic of the Social Democrats—as the higher percentage of the Social Democrat party membership shows. The British Conservative Party only attained its present high standard of organisation after its electoral defeat in 1945.

There are two main types of Socialist party organisation. The French Socialist party is an example of the first type. Its chief characteristic is that it is composed entirely of individual members, who sign a membership form, pay a monthly subscription, and attend local branch meetings. The British Labour Party is the best example of the second type. The party is composed of a mixture of individual members, who join at the local constituency level, and collective members—the Trade Unions and the Co-operatives. The constituency Labour parties—composed of individual members and delegates from the affiliated trade union branches and co-operatives—choose parliamentary candidates and send delegates to the annual conference, where, together with the delegates from the constituencies, they elect the National Executive. The National Executive is composed of seven constituency party members, five union members, twelve members elected by trade union delegates, one member elected by Co-operative and Socialist societies, the Treasurer of the Party, and the Leader and Deputy Leader of the Parliamentary Labour Party, and is responsible for the running of the party outside parliament and for policy statements which are approved by annual conference. However, neither the annual conference nor the National Executive dictates to the Parliamentary Labour Party, which is an autonomous body. In contrast, the French Parliamentary Socialist party (like the Australian Labour party) is subject to the control of the party executive, which is elected by the annual congress. The annual congress is elected, and to a certain extent controlled, by the rank and file at the local branch and federation level.

Just as their organisation has varied, so has the character of Socialist parties differed. The Austrian Socialist party, particularly under the Republic of 1918–34, was a party of 'social integration'. Austrian Socialism was an entire way of life for Austrian workers. Party members were expected to give substantial financial support and to have a deep concern for politics. In return, the party provided education, music (including a series of workers' concerts), drama, travel and holidays, and sport. The great block of flats in the Karl Marx Hof, built free for the workers by the Socialist-controlled Vienna town council, symbolised the intimate link between the workers and the party.[3]

Because they are national rather than strictly working-class parties, the British Labour Party and the Swedish Social Democratic party are less exclusive. Though both are still workers' parties, and there is still a loyalty between workers and the party, the British Labour Party and the Swedish Social Democrats have a large minority following amongst other classes and cannot afford to be tight, closely knit communities of their own. The German Social Democrats have recently changed themselves from a party of integration on the Austrian model to a national party like the British Labour or Swedish Social Democrats.

Democratic Socialists consider that the party system with *competing* political parties is the best way to ensure the possibility of a regular and peaceful change of power and to preserve the basic civil liberties. Socialist governments have come to power under different variations of the party system. Britain, Australia, and New Zealand have predominantly two-party systems, as do the United States and Canada; Western Germany has a three-party system, as does Austria. In France, Sweden, Italy and Holland, there are four or more political parties. These differences in party system reflect both historical differences and differences in electoral methods. France, for example, has not only a broad class division between parties (as is the case in most two-party systems) but also a religious division between religious and anti-religious parties. In addition, the adoption of proportional representation (seats allotted according to total numbers of votes) rather than the 'straight' majority system reinforces tendencies towards a multi-party system.

3 See C. A. Gulick, *Austria from Habsburg to Hitler.* University of California Press, 1948.

Though Democratic Socialists support the idea of competing political parties, there have been times of grave national crisis when they have agreed to join national coalitions. From 1940 to 1945 there was a War Coalition in Britain composed of the Conservative, Labour and Liberal parties; opposition came not from any party but from Members of Parliament not in government. In Austria, the Socialist Party was in coalition with the other main party, the People's Party, from 1945 to 1965. This coalition was formed to prevent a return to the state of near civil war into which pre-war Austrian democracy had degenerated, and to present a united front to the four powers occupying Austria, in particular Soviet Russia. Yet in both cases—in Britain and Austria—the basic freedoms, individual liberty, the rule of law, the right to oppose and criticise were preserved. The British House of Commons, for example, spent two days at a time when British defeat in war seemed imminent, debating whether foreigners in British internment camps were receiving fair treatment. In Sweden, the Social Democrats have been in power, though sometimes in coalition with one of the opposition parties, for thirty years; the opposition is divided and weak. Yet those thirty years have seen the greatest flowering of personal freedom that Sweden has ever known. But Democratic Socialists abhor one-party rule as a permanent ideological principle. Too often one-party rule results in the suppression of personal liberties; the party becomes the chief means of control throughout the state; and all opposition is crushed. To Socialists the normal workings of the party system can only be temporarily abandoned at moments of extreme crisis—and even then the right to oppose, and to resume organised party opposition must be jealously preserved. In an industrial society the best way yet devised to preserve personal rights and liberties is through the constitutional clash of competing political parties.

BUREAUCRACY

In contrast to most governments in the developing countries,

Democratic Socialist governments were fortunate to inherit from previous non-Socialist governments state machines of some degree of efficiency. The bureaucrats or civil servants who ran the state machine were usually obedient to the commands of their new masters. Clement Attlee, commented on the civil servants who carried out the Labour Party's great reforming policies, 'I always found them perfectly loyal.... They carry out the policy of any given government.'[4] The point that Clement Attlee was making was that British civil servants acted constitutionally; they accepted that the 1945 election had given the British Labour government a mandate for change. As a contrast, the German civil service, under the Weimar Republic, acted unconstitutionally because they hampered and impeded the work of Social Democrat and other elected governments; and, then, after the collapse of the Republic, to which they had contributed, they served Hitler with little protest or compunction.

Socialists demand other qualities of civil servants. They should not only carry out the commands of a democratically elected government; they should also see these commands are carried out in as fair and just a way as possible. There should be no riding roughshod over personal liberty, and no attempt to make exceptions to rules in return for a bribe or other favours. Sweden, Denmark and New Zealand have a Ombudsman or Parliamentary Commissioner who is responsible to parliament for safeguarding the individual against bureaucratic abuses and misuse of power. Germany has a similar official to check abuses of power in the army. Britian has that special device, the parliamentary question to a Minister by a Member of Parliament—and now the Labour government has set up a Parliamentary Commissioner to give the individual added protection against bureaucracy.

Bureaucracies should never be allowed to degenerate into a closed élite. The British favour a career civil service which

4 Francis Williams, *A Prime Minister Remembers.* Heinemann, 1961. p. 91.

is open to entry by competitive examination. Though the United States civil service is partly a career service, under the 'spoils system' the winning party brings in many of the top administrators from outside. The American system obviously gains in flexibility; but in the United States the career civil service still lacks the prestige of the French or British civil services. Recently there has been criticism of the British civil service, not for its lack of high professional or ethical standards, but for its inflexibility and resistance to new ideas. In France, for example, where bureaucrats go through a rigorous professional training at the École Nationale d'Administration, there is an overlapping between the bureaucracy, the nationalised industries, and big business. The French civil servant may go through all three during one career; and, as a result, is more flexible and less parochial than his English counterpart. The British Labour government, although they have rejected the American 'spoils system,' have set up a committee to look into the structure, recruitment, training, and management of the Civil Service. Labour wants to ensure that the Civil Service is properly equipped to carry out its crucial role in the administration and direction of the New Britain.

LOCAL GOVERNMENT

In the mid-nineteenth century, Alexis de Tocqueville suggested in *Democracy in America* that one of the two institutions which might prove a counterbalance to the growing power of the industrialised, bureaucratic state, was local self-government.

Most Socialist parties got their first experience of government at the local or provincial government level; and have used local government either as a substitute or more often as a springboard for national advance. The German Social Democrats had gained control of the provincial or land governments long before they formed a national government. Today, though in opposition, they are able, through their control of land and city governments, to influence social conditions in Germany. West Berlin, under its Socialist mayor, Willi Brandt, is a shining example of German Socialism in action. The Austrian Socialists during the ill-fated years of the Austrian Republic were able, through their control of the government of Vienna, to create a little welfare state with ambitious housing, educational, and other social services within the walls of Vienna. The *Canadian Co-operative Commonwealth Federation* (CCF), founded in 1932, created an agrarian welfare state in the Canadian Province of Saskatchewan. Then in 1961 the CCF combined with the Canadian unions to form the *New Democratic Party* which polled over 1 million and 18 per cent of the votes at the 1965 elections.

De Tocqueville's conception of local self-government as a bastion against state power has, in some cases, however, proved unrealisable. Because the prefects are appointed by the central government, French local government has always been highly centralised; while even in Britain, with its long traditions of local self-government, the powers of local government are on the decline. The reason is that many of the social services, such as education and public health, are now more efficiently organised on a national scale. Only in federal states such as Germany, Australia, the United States and Canada, where the power of local regional governments (usually on a much larger scale than British local authorities) are written into the constitution, is local power preserved. Even here it is doubtful whether a regional government is competent to carry on much more than local functions when only the national government can command the resources to finance large-scale development and social services.

The loss of power of the local units of government is not necessarily harmful. It is not at all certain that smaller units of government are naturally more sensitive to the rights and liberties of individuals than a democratically controlled central government—as the example of some of the Southern states of the United States shows. In any case, as the next chapter illustrates, there are other institutions equally suited to act as a bastion to central government. Democratic Socialists believe that people should take part and show interest in their local community; that local government is an essential training in grass-roots democracy; but that it is not necessarily harmful if some vital services such as education are dealt with nationally.

6 Trade Unions and Co-operatives

Democratic Socialists believe that independent, voluntary organisations like trade unions, co-operatives, and professional and religious bodies are an essential part of democracy. The Democratic Socialist ideal is not an absolute concentration of power in the hands of the government but a diffusion of power and ownership. In the words of the 1951 Frankfurt Declaration of the Socialist International, 'Trade Unions and organisations of producers and consumers are necessary elements in a democratic society; they should never be allowed to degenerate into the tools of a central bureaucracy or into a rigid corporative system.'

This chapter is devoted to a discussion of the two voluntary institutions—the Trade Union and the Co-operative—which have contributed most to the advance of Democratic Socialism.

Trade Unions

ORIGINS

The only strength of the exploited industrial workers of nineteenth century Europe lay in their numbers. But this could only be made effective through organisation. In Britain and Sweden, though not in every European country, the first mass-organisation of the working-classes was the Trade Union, or the organisation of men according to their trade or job. After the repeal of the British Combination Laws in 1825, small local unions sprang up in London and the industrial North. A significant development in the early 1830s was the amalgamation of local unions, particularly in the cotton and building industries, to form national unions. In 1834 some of these unions combined to form one central union—the 'Grand National Consolidated Trades Union', with Robert Owen as President. This over-ambitious attempt at centralisation collapsed, however, under pressure from the government and employers. The most notorious government prosecution, the prelude to the attack on the unions, was that of six Dorchester farm labourers, the 'Tolpuddle Martyrs', who were sentenced in 1834 to transportation to Australia for the offence of administering unlawful oaths in the course of their attempt to establish a Friendly Society of Agricultural Labourers as a section of the Grand National. In the third quarter of the nineteenth century, against a background of rising prosperity, the British trade unions became more firmly established on a national basis. The Amalgamated Society of Engineers was founded in 1851, the Amalgamated Society of Carpenters and Joiners in 1860, and, in 1868, the Trades Union Congress was set up. The keynote of this period in British unionism was the emergence of craft unions or unions catering for skilled workers, as the leaders of the movement. In the 1880s, however, unionism became much stronger. In 1889 the miners' union formed a regular central organisation, and unskilled workers, influenced by socialist ideas, began to combine as well. Meanwhile, during the 1870s and '80s, other European workers had formed trades unions.

PURPOSE

The primary purpose of trade unions has always been to improve the wages and working conditions of their members. The first and most basic way of securing this was by collective bargaining. By bargaining together, the members of a trade union ensure that the employer cannot offer their job at a lower price to other, non-trade union, workers, and force the employer to take their interests into consideration. The ultimate deterrent that collective bargaining rests on is the ability of the workers to strike by withdrawing their labour simultaneously. It was by the use of the strike weapon that trade unions forced the employers to recognise their right to bargain on behalf of the workers; it is by the threat of a strike that they are able, in favourable conditions, to compel employers to concede wage advances and improvements in working conditions. Today, however, strikes are few and far between, and most disputes are settled through normal negotiating machinery.

LINKS WITH SOCIALIST PARTIES

By 1900, the trade unions found that, though their primary purpose was collective bargaining, this, by itself, was not enough. In some countries, trade unions were still refused legal recognition; and even in Great Britian, where the climate of opinion was more favourable to the idea of trade unionism, the 1901 judgement by the House of Lords on the Taff Vale case, when the Lords ruled that employers could sue for damages from trade union funds, threatened the legal use of the strike by the unions. There was another reason why action by the trade unions alone was not enough. Under the traditional political and economic system, with unemployment, poverty, and inequality as part of the accepted order of things, the share of income going to wage earners (before tax) fell from about 50 per cent in 1860 to about 40 per cent in 1935.[1] The only way the unions could proportionately improve wages and conditions was by taking political action to change the economic system in their favour.

There were, however, mixed opinions among trade unionists of the early twentieth century as to the form political action should take. In France, most of the leaders of the General Worker's Confederation (C.G.T.), formed in 1895, advocated the use of the general strike, partly because of their organisational and numerical weakness and partly because of their distrust of the divided French Socialist movement, as an alternative to working through the political system. These French trade unionists believed that by the use of the general strike

1 *See* Jay, *Socialism in the New Society.* p. 182.

the ruling classes and capitalists would be brought to their knees; and that the workers would then, themselves, take over the factories and exercise such social discipline as was necessary through the unions. This doctrine was called syndicalism. The result was a series of spectacular strikes in France leading to the 1910 railway strike, which the government broke by calling up the strikers and sending them to work. In Italy, Spain, and to a much lesser extent in Britain (where industrial relations were very bitter between 1910–14 and 1920–26), syndicalist doctrines proved attractive.

Syndicalism failed because the general strike as a revolutionary weapon was inadequate. It was very difficult to organise and maintain, and had little effect on a strong government's control of power. What could strikers do against armed troops? In any case the existence of democratic institutions (or the possibility of them) in most Western European countries made revolutionary means unnecessary. Trade unions decided that a Socialist party which could achieve power by constitutional means provided a more effective way of changing the existing system.

Most European Socialist parties, particularly those most successful electorally, are based on the organised industrial working-classes. As shown in Chapter 1, the British Labour Party was actually started by an alliance between the Socialist political societies and the trade unions—and, to begin with, its membership strength came from trade union support. Although, since then, the Labour Party has become much more the political expression of trade unionism, the unions have always had close ties with it. The party constitution gives the trade unions a built-in strength of twelve out of twenty-eight places on the Labour Party's national Executive Committee and eight votes in every ten at party conferences; and most of the Labour Party funds come from the union's affiliation fees collected through the political levy. But this strong constitutional and financial position has not meant that the Labour Party is merely an appendage of the trade union movement.

There has never been a trade union Prime Minister; only 127 out of the 363 Labour Members of Parliament in the 1966 Parliament were trade union sponsored.

The Swedish Social Democrat Party is the nearest continental equivalent to the British Labour Party. Though there are no formal constitutional links between the trade unions and the party, 60 per cent of the party membership is collectively affiliated, through union branches, to local parties. Thus the Swedish trade unions have always had a strong influence on the Social Democrats—but their relationship is one of partnership. Though it was the Social Democrat governments of the 1930s which first inspired Swedish employers and trade unions to work out the enlightened system of industrial relations which was formally enshrined in the Basic Agreement of 1938, the Social Democrat Government has not intervened directly in questions of wages policy. The German and Austrian trade union movements also support their respective Socialist parties, but individually rather than collectively. Though nearly all the leaders of the German Trade Union Federation, the Deutscher Gewerkschaftsbund (D.G.B.), and the Austrian Trade Union Federation (Ö.G.B.) are Social Democrats, as are the majority of the trade union membership, in both countries, union leaders cannot tie themselves too closely to the Socialist party for fear of alienating the large minority of their membership who have connections with the Catholic or religious parties.

Some European trade union movements are split. In France and Italy the trade union movement is predominantly Communist. The union centres connected with the S.F.I.O. and the P.S.D.I. are the weakest. The largest central trade union organisation in France, the C.G.T., has been controlled by the Communists since 1947, while the Italian General Confederation of Labour (C.G.I.L.) has been Communist controlled (though with Nenni Socialist participation) since 1949. The Communist led unions belong to the Communist controlled World Federation of Trade unions (W.F.T.U.); while most of the Socialist unions have joined the International Confederation of Free Trade Unions (I.C.F.T.U.), which, in disgust at Communist attempts to undermine their authority, split off from the W.F.T.U. in 1949. In France and Italy, there are also strong Catholic unions, though the French Catholic union has now become undenominational. In West Germany the Catholic union trade union movement is dwarfed by the six-million strong D.G.B..

STRUCTURE AND MEMBERSHIP

Trade union structure varies from country to country. In Sweden, for example, the basic organisation is the 'industrial' or industry-wide union. In Great Britain, the pattern is less logical. There are four different types of union. The industrial union; the huge general union (like the Transport and General Workers' and the Municipal and General Workers' unions, with about 1.5 million and 800,000 members respectively), which organise workers in a wide variety of jobs; the occupational union, for example, the Transport Salaried Staffs Association; and the 'craft' union. The difficulty in the fourth category of union is that skills change; in 1958, 366 unions in Britain out of a total of 657, had fewer than 1,000 members and contained only 1 per cent of total membership.

Trade union organisation has a democratic basis. There is a democratic chain of command running from the shop floor through the branch and district organisation to the union headquarters. There are, however, variations in election procedure. Some unions elect all their officials at regular intervals, while in others the minor officials are appointed rather than elected. All union leaders, however, are responsible to their members for their conduct of affairs. In union democracy, there is a danger that apathy can lead to the capture of power by unrepresentative minorities at badly attended branch meetings. Fortunately the democratic principle means that the majority can alway be roused against the minority.

The relationship between the individual unions and the central union organisation varies. The Swedish Trades Union Confederation (*Landsorganisationen i Sverige*—L.O.) has greater power over the individual unions than the British Trades Union Congress (T.U.C.). The Swedish L.O. is, therefore, able to speak effectively for all its members during the central wage bargaining with the employers, and can be certain that, within limits, a central agreement will be respected by the individual unions. Strong power at the centre makes for a more effective trade union movement.

CHANGING ROLE

Though their function is still basically to improve the wages and working conditions of their members, the power and influence of the unions in Britain is now such that Churchill, called them 'an estate of the realm'. There are two reasons for this change. First, the necessities of the 1939–45 war forced all democratic leaders to take the unions into their confidence. Churchill appointed Ernest Bevin, secretary of the most powerful British union, the Transport and General Workers' Union, to the key post of Minister of Labour in his coalition government of 1940–45. Bevin later became Foreign Secretary in the Attlee administration. Secondly, the era of full employment and social justice, brought about by the reforms of the 1940s, has given trade union leaders far greater bargaining power. From being outside and against society, the trade unions have forced governments to accept them as part of the 'Establishment'. The result is that the trade unions are gradually accepting new responsibilities and functions.

In many democratic countries the unions are beginning to influence decisions about the day-to-day life of the workers which formerly used to be the prerogative of management. The unions now have a say in the organisation of work, pay differentials, promotion policy, and even the right of deciding whom and how many to employ. For example, the Swedish L.O., the most powerful of European union organisations, by

fixing a whole series of central agreements with the employers
has achieved a dominant role in the control of industrial
relations. The 1938 Basic Agreement laid down machinery
and procedures for the settlement of industrial disputes; the
1942 Agreement covered accident prevention and industrial
safety; the 1944 Agreement set up a council to promote appren-
tice training in industry; the 1946 Agreement, revised in 1958,
established a system of works councils; the 1948 Agreement
set up machinery and procedure to supervise work study;
while the 1951 Agreement set up a Joint Committee on the
employment of women in industry. During this period there
has been a striking reduction in time lost through stoppages
of work in Sweden; between 1950 and 1963 an average of
only fifty days per year per 1,000 workers was lost. For the
same period the average time lost in Britain was 240 days
per year per 1,000 workers; while the average time lost in the
United States was 1,350 days per year per 1,000 workers.

Since 1945, the unions have played a much greater role in
the shaping of overall economic policy than ever before. In
Sweden, the L.O. nominates two representatives to the
National Labour Market Board, which is directly responsible
for implementing the full employment policies of the Social
Democrat government.[2] In Britain, trade union leaders were
closely consulted about economic policy during the Labour
administrations of 1945–51; a Conservative government in-
vited the union leaders to sit on the National Economic
Development Council to work out, together with representatives of the employers and the government, plans for economic growth.

Now the unions are being drawn into the shaping of what
is known as incomes policy (see Chapter 7 for discussion of
this problem). The classic example of union power in the
shaping of incomes policy is that of the Swedish wage negotiation system. Swedish incomes policy is, in fact, shaped by

2 J. Cooper, *Industrial relations: Sweden shows the way.* Fabian Soc.,
1963.

the central wage negotiations between the L.O. and the Swedish Employers' Confederation (S.A.F.) without direct government interference. These wage negotiations result in a framework agreement lasting one or two years, which lays down the level of earnings increases to be aimed at by the individual unions in negotiation with their respective employers' association. Though there is still substantial 'wages drift'—or wage increases that take place over and above the nationally negotiated wage rates—and the central bargaining is sometimes in danger of becoming a base upon which the wage advances obtained by the piece-rate workers set the pace for the rest of industry, the Swedish wage negotiations represent a serious attempt to grapple with the problem of price inflation. What makes centralised negotiations possible is the enlightened economic and social policy of the Social Democrats; but much of the long-term thinking about incomes policy comes from the unions. The unions have, for some time, been pursuing an active policy of incomes equalisation and job evaluation so that work of a similar nature should cost the same for all employers. As part of this policy, the Swedish unions advocate structural reforms in industry; and, to make labour more mobile, better redundancy pay and vocational training.

The two preceding paragraphs show that the unions are acquiring new functions—a development which could change some of their traditional ones. Yet it is desirable that the unions should, in the last resort, remain independent of government. This is shown most clearly by the loss of power which the unions have experienced in most Communist countries. In most Communist countries the unions are, in effect, completely controlled by the state. They are mere government departments; and, since the government is also the employer, they have degenerated into little more than employers' organisations for maintaining discipline, preventing strikes, raising production and cutting costs.

The trade unions helped the advance of Democratic Socialism in many ways. The control of the affairs of a trade union is, in itself, a democratic education. As the Oxford lecturer in industrial relations, Allan Flanders, has put it, in his book *Trade Unions*, 'As compared with the trade union there is probably no other institution in the country which brings as many people into voluntary or part-time service on behalf of their fellows and gives them a first-hand experience of the democratic methods of administration.' The unions have also helped to secure a better standard of living and higher status for the workers both by their own efforts and by their support of Socialist parties. Finally, by their independence—even when Socialist governments are in power—the unions provide an essential part of the framework of democratic institutions.

SPECIAL CASE: ISRAEL

The Israeli trade union movement, the Histadruth, is very much a case on its own. Whereas the European trade unions were based on the industrial working-class, the Histadruth (founded in 1920) was based on the agricultural workers and agricultural co-operatives and was from the first much more than an organisation for collective bargaining.

In 1922 the League of Nations formally confirmed the establishment of a British mandate over Palestine which included the putting into effect of the Declaration by the British Government in 1917 in favour of the establishment of a 'National Home' for the Jewish people. The British authorities, however, remained preoccupied with law and order and did little to develop the country's poor natural resources. So there were no industries and no industrial workers. The Jews themselves were forced to pioneer the country's development (one of their early pioneers, A. D. Gordon, wrote, 'We are not going to change anything or improve anything. We are going to begin from the beginning.') and carry out for themselves many of the functions of government. Most of these they exercised through the Histadruth.

The Histadruth started its own business enterprises to give

employment to Jews and today controls a large number of successful firms; 60 per cent of the economy of Israel, which became independent in 1948, is now controlled by either the State, the Histadruth or the Co-operative movement. The Histadruth set up its own welfare services, including a comprehensive health scheme, which it still runs to day. The Histadruth also provides workers' housing; and helps the government in the financing of public investment.[3]

Three-quarters of Israel's agricultural and industrial workers are members of the Histadruth, while there is substantial 'white-collar' membership as well: members subscribe directly to it rather than to their own separate unions which merely receive a proportion of the total affiliation payments. First loyalty is to the Histadruth. In return, it has won for them the acceptance of the principle that agricultural and industrial workers are entitled to a standard of living equal to that of any other Israeli citizen. The dominant Socialist party in Israel, Mapai, is far more a trades unions' party than the British Labour Party. Like Mapam and Ahdut Ha'avoda, the two other Socialist parties, Mapai participates in the work of the Histadruth. Until the 1965 Histadruth elections, there were two party systems: the national one, including all the political parties, and the Histadruth system comprising only the Socialists. Now, though the Socialists still remain dominant, the anti-Socialist coalition have 15.2 per cent of the seats. Though there are sometimes conflicts of interest between the government and the Histadruth, particularly over wages policy, no important Cabinet decision is taken without consulting the Histadruth. Histadruth is perhaps the most powerful trade union movement (though not, of course, the biggest) in the world; and its power and its ability to secure a high standard of living for its workers come as much from its own efforts as from the government.

3 *See* Margaret Plunkett, 'The Histadruth'. *Industrial and Labour Relations Review*, 1958.

Co-operatives

ORIGINS

The co-operative owed its birth to the inspiration of Robert Owen. When Robert Owen started his search for a better way of life, he turned first to the co-operative idea. 'Competition', he wrote, 'must be replaced by co-operation.' To this end, he established a series of self-sufficient, self-governing communities, practising the co-operative way of life in England, Ireland, North America and Mexico. But none of these communities was really successful. Lack of capital, sufficient agricultural or industrial expertise, and the difficulty which men find in living together, broke them all. Even his 'Labour Exchange', set up in 1832 in the Gray's Inn Road, London, as the first experiment in consumer co-operation failed. At the Labour Exchange, articles were exchanged at the estimate of the value of the labour which had gone into their production. Unfortunately the collapse of the trade unions movement in the 1830s removed the backing for Owen's experiment. But though Owen's practical experiments in co-operation failed, his ideas bore fruit.

The first successful exercise in co-operation came just before the industrial boom of the 1850s in Britain. In 1844 twenty-eight men from Rochdale in Lancashire (mostly flannel weavers) founded the Rochdale Equitable Pioneers Co-operative Society. The ultimate aim of this body was the establishment 'as soon as practicable' of a self-supporting society on Owenite lines. But, as a first step, the Rochdale pioneers set up a highly successful consumer store. The origins of the world consumer co-operative movement spring from this Rochdale store.

The object of this store was not to make profits for shareholders as in a private company but to sell reliable goods at reasonable prices, distributing surplus earnings among the members. Most of the profits, after provision had been made for future investment, were distributed to members by a dividend worked out in proportion to their purchases, not to their shareholding. Members subscribed capital but there was an upper limit to the amount each might contribute, and interest was paid at a fixed and low rate. Each member, irrespective of his capital contribution, had one vote.

During the 1850s and 1860s, against a background of increasing prosperity, similar co-operative societies began to spring up all over the country. In 1863, the first Co-operative Wholesale Society was set up to buy goods for the local co-operatives. By the 1880s, the Co-operative Wholesale Society started to manufacture its own goods too.

CONSUMER CO-OPERATION TODAY

Today the British Consumer Co-operative movement controls 11 per cent of the total retail trade in Britain, has some thirteen million members (about a quarter of the total population) and has been the pioneer of important innovations in retailing, including the self-service store, although in recent years British Co-operative retailing, as a whole, has begun to fall behind the best private firms. Consumer co-operation has spread to all Western European countries, but has developed less rapidly outside Europe except in India, the Middle Western States of the United States, Japan, and Cyprus. There are flourishing consumer co-operative movements in France (with three million members), Western Germany (with just under three million), Austria and Scandinavia. Special mention should be made of the Swedish consumer co-operative movement, which does 12 per cent of the total retail trade in the country, has some 3 million members (or more than a third of the Swedish population), and acts as front runner for Swedish retailing in price, quality, style and standard of management.

PRINCIPLES OF CONSUMER CO-OPERATION[4]

1. *Members ultimately control their society on the basis of one*

4 *See* Crosland's brilliant essay 'The Principles of Co-operation' (included in his *The Conservative Enemy*) originally published as Chapter 2 of the Co-operative Independent Commission Report.

member, one vote. It is this democratic principle that distinguishes a co-operative trading organisation both from an ordinary capitalist enterprise where control is based on the size of the capital holding and from a state-controlled marketing enterprise.

2. *The profit or 'surplus' is distributed to members as a dividend on purchases.* In contrast to private enterprise, the profit belongs to the consumer; and it accrues to him in proportion to his purchases instead of to the property owner in proportion to his shareholding. The British Co-operative Independent Commission, set up by the Co-operative Union (the movement's advisory centre) to examine the workings of the movement, and chaired by Hugh Gaitskell shortly before he became Leader of the Labour Party, calculated that the payment of dividend on purchases distributed £50 million a year to ordinary consumers, which might otherwise have gone to a smaller class of property owners.

3. *Members who are capital owners receive only a fixed return on the capital.* The capital owners are in the position of preference shareholders receiving a fixed rate of interest, and with no claim to the residual profit which goes to the consumer. The fact that the consumer co-operative movement does not distribute its profits as an equity income to ordinary shareholders, but pays instead a fixed return on share capital which is not transferable, is the major contribution of the consumer co-operative movement towards a fairer distribution of national income. The Gaitskell Commission calculated that, if the annual dividend and share interest paid out to consumers was, in fact, paid to private enterprise shareholders as a dividend on ordinary shares, the result would be very large capital gains for a small body of shareholders. The co-operative movement therefore, in the words of the Gaitskell Commission, creates 'the possibility of achieving economic growth without a continuous rise in the value of privately owned property.'

4. *The duty of a co-operative society must be to conduct its*

trading operations so that consumers are not merely negatively protected against exploitation, but derive the greatest possible benefit from the existence of a co-operative movement. This implies that the retail society should sell at prices which are never consistently undercut by any major competitor; always sell goods of the highest quality; maintain the highest standard of shop location, layout, appearance and service; and generally act as the watchdog of the consumer. The aggressive competitiveness of the Swedish Co-operative Union and Wholesale Society (K.F.) has often been responsible for breaking up monopolies and bringing down prices. In 1928 the K.F., with the support of other Scandinavian co-operative movements, decided to break the monopoly held by the General Electric Company over electric light bulbs. So they built their own factory at Luma in Sweden and forced the price of bulbs down 37 per cent. A more recent example is in the washing powder market. Here K.F. took over the German Henkel factory and shortly afterwards the price of this factory's most important product, Persil, was reduced by a total of 22 per cent.

STRUCTURE OF CONSUMER CO-OPERATION

Consumer co-operation is still based on the autonomous local society which may own only one or two shops (if it is a village society) or at the other end of the scale control a large central store with a great number of branches (as in Birmingham or London). In Britain more than a third of the societies still have fewer than 2,000 members each, but over two-thirds of the members belong to the 140 societies which have more than 20,000 members. The members of the society elect the management committee from amongst themselves at the annual general meeting, and hold quarterly meetings to receive reports on the conduct of the society and its financial and trading position, and to give an opportunity for criticism and discussion. Today the complexity of the medium or large sized co-operative society forces the management committee to delegate the detailed day-to-day management of the society to trained, full-time, professional officials; and the growth of the co-operative movement has meant that only a small minority of the total membership actually attend the meetings of their society. This is not disastrous so long as the inactive majority remember that they still retain their full democratic power and can exercise it whenever they choose. The danger arises when apathy allows unrepresentative but well organised minorities to get control—as has happened in a few British societies.

Most local British societies belong to the Co-operative Wholesale Society which buys wholesale for them or produces the goods they sell to their members. Local co-operative societies also support the Co-operative Union which acts as the movement's policy making and advisory centre and includes legal, statistical, educational and publicity departments. The highest authority in the co-operative union is the Co-operative Congress which has become the annual parliament of the co-operative movement, The Swedish co-operative movement combines the administrative and trading centres in a single organisation (K.F.). The Administrative Council of the K.F. which supervises policy questions, but leaves the day-to-day detail to the K.F.'s board of directors, is elected by a district congress of local co-operative societies. The final sanction on K.F.'s policies is held by the Annual National Congress of district representatives.

The Swedish K.F. is politically neutral. The British co-operative movement, however, is closely connected with the Labour Party. The Co-operative Union is represented equally with it on the National Council of Labour; while the Co-operative Party, which is supported by funds from local societies, and during the 1914–18 war put up independent candidates for parliament, now puts forward candidates for parliament jointly with the Labour party.

PRODUCERS' CO-OPERATIVES

There is another, quite different, type of co-operation—the

producers' co-operative. Producers' co-operatives range from society which give common credit, marketing co-operatives in Japan, France and East Africa, to highly sophisticated, self-sufficient co-operative farms in Israel.

Producers' co-operatives have so far been confined almost entirely to agriculture. Though the consumer's co-operatives have been extremely successful in running large-scale production of consumer goods, these concerns have been managed on the lines of ordinary business enterprises. The co-operative workshop (where the workers are entirely their own masters) is confined in Britain to clothing, boots and shoes, and printing, where the economic unit is comparatively small. Large scale industrial production makes workers' control in the traditional sense very difficult. The same is true of large scale prairie-type agriculture with a small population working large areas of land.

The most interesting development of voluntary producer co-operation is found in Israel.[5] Early Jewish immigrants believed that only by settling as workers on the land could they effectively establish themselves in Palestine. In Turkish Palestine of the 1900s, and later under the British mandate, the Jews' lack of private capital made co-operation a necessity. Land was bought by the Jewish National Fund, a body set up for the purpose, which leased it to those Jewish settlers without capital who wished to set up as co-operators. The Fund continued to help them financially after they were established on the land.

Of the three main types of Israeli agricultural co-operatives, the oldest is the *Kibbutz*. It is the most complete form of voluntary co-operation in the world. Not only is the entire agricultural economy of the co-operative collectively organised and managed, but living is communal as well. The Kibbutz caters collectively for all the needs of its members including

5 The Russian collective farm, the kolkhoz, is a compulsory rather than voluntary organisation.

housing, food, clothes, and the education of children. There is
no private property. The first Israeli Kibbutz was started at
Degania in 1909 by Socialists from Eastern Europe.

The *Moshav* settlement was founded in 1921 by Jews who
believed in co-operation but were unable to reconcile themselves to the full demands of the Kibbutz. The Moshav has
been much more popular with the new Jewish immigrants
from the Arab countries, and with Jews from Eastern Europe
to whom the Kibbutz seemed too similar to a Communist
collective to be attractive. In the Moshav, land is allotted to
each family and farmed separately. The family also lives
separately. But the supplies of seed, fertilisers and agricultural
implements, the marketing of the products of the Moshav,
and the provision of essential services such as education,
health and sanitation, are organised co-operatively.

The *Moshav Shitufi*, the third main form of agricultural co-
operative, only developed since 1948, combines the characteristics of the Kibbutz and the Moshav. In the Moshav Shitufi
the family lives separately but farms collectively. Agricultural
co-operation in Israel is more than just an economic exercise.
It was from the first a conscious attempt to put Socialist
principles into practice. In the Kibbutz or Moshav there is no
rigid hierarchy; in theory, at least, all are equal. Each member
of a Kibbutz or a Moshav has to take part in deciding the
policy of his co-operative. He receives 'grass roots' training in
democratic participation.

The universal applicability of Israeli co-operation should
not, however, be exaggerated. Precisely because it was as
much a political as an economic exercise, Israeli co-operation
demands a certain degree of political and social sophistica-
tion; and it is revealing that the relative share of the co-
operatives in the Israeli economy has declined.

CO-OPERATION AND DEMOCRATIC SOCIALISM

The co-operatives—consumer and producer—have helped the
cause of Democratic Socialism by giving their members an

education in democracy. Consumer co-operatives have provided the workers with cheap and good quality consumer goods; and by their system of giving only a fixed return of capital have helped to bring about a fairer distribution of national wealth. Above all the co-operatives are a working example of the Democratic Socialist ideal of a diffused and responsible pattern of ownership.

7 Agenda for Affluence

THE AFFLUENT SOCIETY
A product of the reforms pioneered by Socialist and left-wing governments in the 1930s and 1940s and of the rapid pace of technological change that characterises the second stage of industrialism, the affluent society of the 1960s and 1970s poses problems that are different in kind from the problems of the 1930s. To meet the challenge of the new society, Socialists have to shape an entirely new set of policies that reinterpret their principles in the light of the new conditions.

The triumph of affluence in the West is not yet complete. Old-style poverty and social injustice still exist. The main reason for this is that most Socialist governments did not remain in power long enough to carry out their plans in full; and their reforms were either partially undermined or not developed by the conservative governments which succeeded them. The United States, which has never had a major Socialist party, provides the most striking mixture of affluence and poverty. *The Affluent Society*, the work of the distinguished American economist Professor J. K. Galbraith, draws a contrast between the private affluence of the majority of Americans and the inadequacies of their public services. There is no comprehensive system of medical care; and in spite of the high standard of living, one in thirteen Americans lives on the edge of poverty. Thirteen years of Conservative rule in Britain produced a considerable backlog of badly needed reforms which included bringing the social services up to date, in particular old age pensions, housing and education, the introduction of effective economic planning machinery, and making the taxation system a more effective means of redistribution. But Sweden, which has had thirty-four years of Social Democrat government, shows that a determined Socialist government can effectively abolish poverty by economic planning, get rid of glaring social injustices by a comprehensive and ambitious system of social services, and promote equality by redistributive taxation and a just educational system.

Despite the existence of old-style poverty and social injustice, the contours of the affluent society are already apparent. Its characteristics are a high general level of prosperity, and a rapid rate of scientific and technological change. Socialist reforms laid the foundation of a new affluence. Control of the economy brought full employment and steady economic advance; in addition the introduction of a system of social services and redistributive taxation has ensured that the fruits of full employment are more evenly shared. The result has been a striking advance in prosperity throughout Western Europe, North America, and Australasia. Even in Britain, which under the Conservatives had one of the worst growth rates in Europe, average net incomes rose by 25 per cent and average personal expenditure by 23 per cent in the ten years after 1951. The main social consequences of affluence have been a growing equality in consumption (cars and television sets are no longer luxuries but are becoming universal necessities); an increase in population caused by improved medical services, better housing, a higher proportion of married women and a greater readiness to have larger families; and, as a result of educational reforms and a changing work force, a modified social structure.

The pace of scientific and technological change has become increasingly rapid. Harold Wilson, speaking at the 1963 Labour Party conference said, 'It is, of course, a cliché that we are living at a time of such rapid change that our children are accepting as part of their everyday life things which would have been dismissed as science fiction a few years ago.' Within fifty years man's way of life has been revolutionised. Electric power has completely changed production techniques; the motor and the aeroplane have altered conceptions of distance and time; telephone, wireless and television bring instant communications; and nuclear power threatens man's survival. In the next twenty years, automation will change the face of industry. The revolutionary nature of automation, in the words of Harold Wilson, is 'that it replaces the hitherto unique human functions of memory and of judgment.'

The affluent society throws up new problems; and new opportunities. Prosperity and technical change give rise to new economic and social difficulties; but also provide a chance to humanise work and increase leisure. The crowded conurbations and the increase in car ownership threaten to ruin man's environment but could offer a new standard in social amenities. The growth in mass communications, which has disturbing cultural implications, could, in fact, enlarge cultural values. Similarly, technical advance represents both a threat to democratic institutions and a unique opportunity of widening them. The task that faces Democratic Socialists is how best to harness the potentialities of the affluent society so that the peoples of the Western world are able to live in greater freedom and equality.

THE POLITICAL CHALLENGE

The end of the 1939–45 war saw the first real triumph of Democratic Socialism. In 1946, Britain, France, Belgium, Holland, Austria, Switzerland, Italy, Norway, Sweden, Denmark, Australia and New Zealand were governed by Socialist parties or left-wing coalitions. The same was true of Eastern Europe. By 1950 Eastern Europe, except Yugoslavia, was under Soviet rule. By 1952, Socialist parties had fallen from power in Britain, France, Belgium, Denmark, Australia and New Zealand. Judged as a whole, the 1950s was a decade of Conservatism.

After the war, the mood of the electorate in most Western

countries had been radical. They wanted a better world with
full employment and less social injustice. The Socialist reforms
of the 1940s blunted this radicalism. The peoples of the West
began to take full employment and the welfare state for
granted. Inflation replaced unemployment as the main
domestic threat; while Socialist governments became identified
with the high taxation, rationing, controls and austerity which
was an inevitable feature of the immediate post-war world.
The main enemy was Communism—still considered by some
West European electorates as the natural ally of Socialism.
For all these reasons people voted Right. There were exceptions: the Swedish Social Democrats and the Norwegian
Labour party continued in power and the Danish Social
Democrats returned to office in 1953. But the British Labour
Party, seriously split on policy, was out of office for thirteen
years; the German Social Democrats, whose electoral chances
were damaged by the 'cold war', have not formed a single
government under the Western German Republican régime;
the French Socialists, who had made bad mistakes, were
relegated to impotence by General de Gaulle's coup d'état;
and, in Australasia, the New Zealand Labour party alone had
a short spell in government after 1957. The Australian Labour
Party has been in opposition since 1949.

Conservative governments—in Britain, France, Germany
and Italy, Australia and New Zealand—had to accept full
employment and the welfare state. Their rule was characterised, however, by a reversal of the trend towards greater
equality. Thus they put more of the financial burden of the
social services on the backs of the workers; and it was the
business-classes that gained most from full employment.
Conservative governments also turned a blind eye to the
implications of the affluent society. For a time, the peoples
of the Western democracies were content to enjoy the new
experience of prosperity. The old class hatreds were soothed
by affluence. The class solidarity of poorly paid manual
workers was modified by the growth in personal incomes, by

the increase of comparatively well paid white-collar workers, and by reforms in the educational system which opened up new ladders of advancement for working-class children.

So affluence presented Socialist parties with a formidable challenge. To achieve power they had to create new policies to deal with the problems of affluence. They got little help from traditional Socialist thinkers. Early Socialists had supposed that once solutions to the basic problems of production and distribution had been found, man's life would be a kind of earthly paradise. The Swedish Social Democrat, Per Albin Hansson, put the dilemma, 'We have had so many victories that we are in a difficult position. A people with political liberty, full employment, and social security has lost its dreams.' Fortunately opposition threw up a new generation of Socialist leaders who began the shaping of new policies. In Britain, for example, first Hugh Gaitskell and then Harold Wilson gave the Labour Party a new dynamic. Wilson's speech at the 1963 Party Conference revealed that the Labour Party understood the problems posed by the affluent society. Inevitably, *The New Britain*, Labour's manifesto for the 1964 election, had to deal with the many omissions of thirteen years of Conservative rule; but it also contained imaginative policies to meet the needs of the new age. The Labour Party's massive victory at the 1966 election, following its narrow victory in 1964, showed that the British people found its programme relevant. Labour established new support among the technical classes—scientists, technicians, engineers, architects, and managers; and, despite, its preoccupation with Britain's economic difficulties, could become the permanent majority party. In 1966, the German Social Democrats, though still in opposition, were making the running in German politics. In Italy, where Socialists have had little influence on events, the two Socialist parties were partners in the Centre Left Coalition, and in 1964, for the first time, a Socialist President was elected. In France, the Socialists are leading the emerging opposition to the one-man rule of de Gaulle. The European stage is being cleared for a new series of Socialist reforms.

ECONOMIC STRATEGY

The overriding problem of the free market economy was mass unemployment. The overriding problems of the affluent economy are price inflation and structural unemployment.

Full employment has given the trade unions much greater power. In the full employment economy, the trade unions have been able to demand substantial pay increases—often in excess of productivity—without fear of their members being thrown out of work. To preserve their original profit margins, the employers have pushed up prices. The result has tended to be an inflationary spiral. Though a small amount of inflation does little harm if the economy is expanding at a reasonable rate, prices continuously rising at more than four per cent a year force workers to demand more money in wages to maintain their position before the price rise. Those on fixed incomes—such as old age pensioners—suffer, the country's exports lose their competitiveness, and damage is done to economic growth.

Socialists have attempted to tackle the problem of cost inflation (as this type of inflation is called) by planning the growth of incomes. There are two comparatively successful examples of incomes policy. The first is the Swedish system, described in the last chapter, the second is the Dutch system, introduced after the war by the Catholic-Labour coalition. The difference between the two is the degree of government intervention. While under the Swedish system the government only intervenes in an indirect way, the Dutch government is directly involved in incomes policy. Though unions and employers negotiate wage increases independently, wage negotiations have to be approved by the government-appointed Board of Mediators. This is done in the light of forecasts of productivity by the government's Central Planning Bureau, and the social and economic priorities suggested by the Social and Economic Council—a consultative body composed of nominees of the government, trade unions, and employers.

The important feature of Dutch incomes policy has been its

interaction with wider economic and social questions. While the Dutch unions have been prepared to forgo wage increases at times of economic difficulty, thus enabling the government to exercise some control over the size and timing, the government has agreed to wage increases as compensation for policy changes (as, for example, when pension contributions were increased in 1957) and keeps control over other types of income, including profits. In addition, the government has attempted to create a wages structure based on the nature of the work performed.

Both the Dutch and Swedish incomes policy systems are far from perfect. There is still substantial 'wages drift'—or wage increases that take place over and above nationally negotiated wage rates. But the reason the two systems have had any success at all is that the planning of wages takes place against a tough policy on profits and prices, an egalitarian tax and social policy, and some form of economic planning. In the future, most Western Governments will have to introduce an incomes policy. There are many difficulties involved—in particular the question of the independent wage negotiation function of the trade unions. But the Dutch and the Swedes have shown, in their different ways, that cost inflation can be partially overcome.

Technical change of all kinds, in particular automation, presents great economic and social difficulties. In the United States, where automation is most advanced and there is already significant 'structural' unemployment, it has been calculated that forty million new jobs will be needed by 1970. Harold Wilson said at the 1963 Labour Party Conference, 'Since technological progress left to the mechanism of private industry and private property can lead only to high profits for a few, a high rate of employment for a few, and to mass redundancies for the many, if there had never been a case for Socialism before, automation would have created it.'

Employment policy in an age of technological change must be more than just planning for economic expansion. If the 'structural' unemployment caused by technological change is to be overcome, there must be further measures. To encourage mobility of labour between jobs there must be a background of social security. The British Labour government is introducing an ambitious and comprehensive Charter of Rights for all employees; this Charter includes the right to compensation for loss of job, the right to half pay during periods of sickness and unemployment and, above all, the right to retraining for all adult workers. The employment policy of the Swedish Social Democrat government has gone further; the state pays the costs for transporting and rehousing unemployed workers and their families.[1] But mobility of labour between jobs, by itself, is not enough. There must also be a policy of bringing industry to the unemployed. This implies steering private industry to depressed areas; and creating new employment in these areas by setting up government-financed factories and stimulating public works. The British Labour government has made a start by introducing special incentives to encourage investment in depressed areas and also new and more stringent location of industry controls.

Automation presents a new opportunity of humanising work. Despite Socialist reforms, public ownership and a growing social awareness in parts of private industry, work, for the majority of industrial and many white-collar workers, is still boring—both because of the nature of the work and their own lack of status.

In modern mass-production, division of labour often reduces the role of the worker to the minutest cog in the machine. Work is monotonous and tiring. The worker may react to monotony either by falling into apathy or becoming militant. There is a strong correlation between industrial militancy and mass-production—as, for example, in the British car industry. The nature of work also has an effect on the worker's family; the worker may react to the domination of the machine by

1 See *Economic Expansion and Structural Change: A Trade Union Manifesto.*

attempting to dominate his family or by bringing his apathy into the home.[2] Fortunately automation offers a way out. Whereas mass-production reduced a worker from a craftsman to a cog, automation makes him a craftsman again. Automation demands retraining in new skills; and with complex automatic plant, a worker has to make decisions for himself. Provided that governments can ensure the new employment that automation makes necessary, it may well be worthwhile, even from a human point of view, to hasten the process of automation.[3] No Socialist party yet has a policy on work, apart from providing more of it; the fact that automation is now opening up new possibilities for 'job-satisfaction' makes it essential for one to be devised.

Socialists must tackle the complementary question of workers' status in industry. There are definite indications that the workers are not satisfied with present arrangements. In Britain, in the twenty years of full employment since 1940, strikes about matters other than wage increases—including working arrangements, rules and discipline—rose from one third to three-quarters of all stoppages. Dissatisfaction with job-content is paralleled by a desire for increased control over its circumstances.

Any policy on workers' status must, however, have as its central assumption the strength and independence of the unions. In the full employment economy the unions, through their collective bargaining techniques, have significantly increased workers' control in industry. They have extended their power beyond the traditional questions of wages and hours to questions of organisation of work, pay differentials, promotion policy, and even hiring and firing. The unions have achieved these advances in workers' status by their independent power; and though there are common, sometimes overriding, interests, management and workers will continue to represent dif-

2 *See* Richard M. Titmuss, 'Industrialisation and the Family' in his *Essays on the Welfare State*. Allen and Unwin, 1958.
3 *See* Lisl Klein's Fabian pamphlet 'The Meaning of Work', 1963.

ferent sides. The guarantee of the workers' position is a strong union movement which, in the final analysis, remains independent of management.

Any policy to increase the workers' status must operate on two levels; on the level of management, and on the factory floor. Germany offers an interesting example of workers' participation in management. By the German Co-Determination Law of 1952, the German Trade Union Federation secured legal representation in management for the German workers. By the Co-Determination Law, one-third of the supervisory or non-executive board appointed by shareholders must be made up of elected, union-supported, representatives of the employees. Since 1947, German workers have had even greater representation in the coal and steel industries; they elect up to half of the supervisory Board and, together with the unions, appoint one member, the Personnel Director, to the full-time board of management. The German Co-Determination Law has given the German worker power over all management decisions which directly concern him—but most trade union movements would prefer not to get so closely involved with management. Any scheme for workers' participation in management must leave the unions free to improve the workers' status by collective bargaining. On the factory floor level, the job-enlargement that automation brings can give workers more control over the timing of their work. It is the responsibility of Democratic Socialists to work out, together with management and unions, a policy for workers' status and job-content which ensures that the worker enjoys not only the financial but the social and human benefits of the affluent society.

PLANNING THE ENVIRONMENT

Today the urban civilisation, characteristic of the advanced economies, threatens to silt up completely. The great conurbations spread endlessly over the countryside, while city life is being slowly strangled by the motor car.

The spread of the great conurbations—London, Paris, the Ruhr, the cities of Western Netherlands, Milan, and the cities of North America—has three main causes. The first is the attractive power of the cities. Economic activity generates further activity; and people are attracted to the great economic centres by the prospects of higher pay and better amenities. The second is the autonomous decay of the non-metropolitan areas, dependent on declining industries and services, which pushes people to look for work in the metropolitan areas. The third is the growth of population which would, by itself, make the problem of planning a difficult one. The result is congestion at the centre; the growth of suburbs and satellite towns, dependent on the centre; and decay and depopulation in other parts furthest from the conurbations.

In every advanced country car ownership has increased astronomically. In the United States there is one car to every 2·9 people—and within twenty years the Western European countries will reach the same figure. The car saves time and widens horizons, but creates chaos in towns and cities planned and built in the pre-motor stage. In central New York and parts of central London congestion has brought traffic speeds down to about 5 m.p.h. The commercial life of central New York has already begun to decay; between 1948 and 1959 four department stores closed their central New York branches and total retail trade has stagnated. The motor car also damages the quality of city life: citizens are in constant danger from passing motor cars, and noise and fumes are becoming a major social evil.

The only way to ensure that urban man is not overwhelmed by his inventions is by the combination of two different types of planning—by economic planning of jobs, and by environmental planning of houses and transport. Just as it is the role of economic planning to create jobs and produce the resources to pay for houses and transport, so environmental planning should ensure that the jobs, houses, and transport are so organised to provide a decent environment. Environmental

planning is still in its infancy. The British Labour government
of 1945–51 made a brave start. By the New Towns Acts of
1946, they created a series of planned population centres to
prevent suburban sprawl around the big cities. By the Town
and Country Planning Act of 1947 they introduced a system
of physical planning through control of building development.
The Act, for the first time, required local authorities to provide
an overall land-use plan; but through defects in the Act, and
later Conservative amendments, it did not lead to comprehensive modern development of Britain's cities—as the 1963
Buchanan Report on 'Traffic in Towns' showed. Swedish
physical planning, which gives local authorities the right to
buy land at reasonable prices in advance of use, has made
comprehensive development much easier; as a result Stockholm, with the obvious advantage of being a smaller city, is in
less danger of being overwhelmed by the motor car than
London. Today, a more ambitious plan is needed to tackle the
problems of conurbation sprawl and motor congestion. The
British Labour government has, therefore, set up a national
network of Regional Planning Boards. These boards· will
co-ordinate both environmental and economic planning; produce overall plans to separate urban man from the car; and
control the conurbation spread. In addition, there must be
overall national control of the geographical pattern of employment opportunities to prevent further drift to the conurbations. Only by such plans can the physical environment of
the affluent society be made worthy of its economic prosperity.

LEISURE AND CULTURE

The 1959 British Labour policy statement states, 'Once full
employment is again secured, the emphasis will increasingly
be not on jobs for all but on leisure for all—leisure and how
to use it.' The coming of automation has made possible a great
expansion of leisure-time. Obviously how man spends his
leisure is a question only he can answer. Socialists believe,
however, that it is the government's duty to see that there

is a wide field of leisure and cultural activities available to all.

New consumption patterns have ensured that some leisure activities (like watching a television set or driving a motor car) which were formerly the privilege of a few are now available to all. But studies of leisure activities in the United States,[4] where automation is most advanced, has shown that the basing of leisure primarily on the motor car and the television set is not enough. Very often the American worker fills his time by getting a second job. In contrast, the Swedish worker has less difficulty in filling his leisure. Over one in ten Swedes take adult education courses. The high cultural standard is reflected in the quality of the Swedish daily Press; in the design of Swedish consumer goods; and in the fact that far more books are published in Sweden per head of population than in the United States. The productive use made by Swedes of their leisure is the result of many factors, including the excellence of Swedish schools; but part of the credit must go to the progressive attitude of the Social Democrats towards government support of many leisure and cultural activities. The state subsidises many sporting facilities, including athletic tracks and swimming baths; gives financial support to adult education groups; and backs a string of state theatres as well as a state theatrical touring company.[5]

The most immediate cultural decision facing Socialists is the control and use of the 'mass media'—the popular newspapers, radio, television and cinema. One of the results of affluence and technology has been the spectacular growth of the communications industry. The mass media at their best can provide high quality entertainment for leisure and a superb instrument of popular education; at their worst they can have a corrupting effect on cultural standards. The aim should be to ensure a wide choice of newspaper, television and radio programmes, and films catering for minority as well as majority tastes. The

4 *See* David Riesman, *Abundance for What*. Chatto and Windus, 1964.
5 *See* Perry Anderson, *New Left Review*. Jan.–Feb. and May–June 1961.

questions are whether the control of the media by commercial interests provides a wide enough choice; and how to ensure choice without resorting to the type of government control common under dictatorship and in some Communist countries.

Each particular media presents its own problems. A radio and television policy has to ensure that there are a wide variety of programmes appealing to different interests. This is not just a question of a choice of channels. The numerous American radio and television channels, controlled by commercial interests and paid for by advertising revenue, produce programmes of an astonishing lack of variety and quality. An American government official responsible for broadcasting has called American radio and television 'a cultural desert'. The trouble is that commercial television and radio owners are more interested in making money than in providing a public service. The solution, suggested by British and Swedish experience, is competition between independent public corporations, charged with the responsibility of providing a variety of programmes. The British Broadcasting Corporation is paid for by licensing fees collected through the Post Office—. but is entirely independent of government, providing space for all kinds of political and non-political opinion. Competition between different public corporations could provide a wide choice. There is also a place for a television channel devoted entirely to educational purposes, particularly adult education.

In Britain, the structure of the Press is characterised by an unhealthy tendency towards concentration and monopoly. Seven out of eight national morning newspapers in Britain are controlled by one of three groups. The determining factor as to whether a newspaper can survive is not the numbers of readers it can satisfy, but the amount of advertising revenue it can attract. The British Labour government has to prevent further newspaper mergers and devise some way of lessening the dependence of British newspapers on advertising, while preserving the independence of the Press.

Advertising is a challenge in itself. Advertisements can help the consumer by providing him with useful information and bringing down prices. However, there are now many powerful arguments against advertising. Manufacturers waste resources on the costly advertising of almost identical consumer products. And there is also the danger that too many trivial and sometimes downright misleading advertisements will have a detrimental effect on cultural standards.

In the affluent society all governments will have to have a 'leisure' policy. The task of Socialists is to pioneer different methods of expanding leisure and cultural opportunities.

AFFLUENCE AND DEMOCRACY

Harold Wilson in one of his pre-1964 election speeches said 'we want a Britain in which everyone, not a small clique or class, feel themselves to be part of a process of new policy-making, of taking national decisions, where every home, every club, every pub is its own Parliament in miniature—thrashing out the issues of the day'. If democracy is not to become a mask for rule by a few, there must be a genuine participation by the people in the workings of democracy at every level.

Socialist reforms and technical change have not only increased the power of the state; they have also increased the power and influence of the servants of the state—the planners, bureaucrats, technocrats and scientists. The danger is that key decisions will be taken by these and other groups, like the controllers of the mass-communications system, without either the elected representatives or the people themselves being aware that they have been taken. The elected representatives of the people may be ill-equipped to question complex and technical decisions in parliament—if they ever get to hear about them. For the majority of the population, Socialist reforms have taken the heat out of politics. Enjoying their prosperity, they are in danger of becoming apathetic, and allowing affairs to be run without their participation.

If the affluent society presents certain threats to democratic institutions, it also introduces strong compensating factors. The most important of these is the growth of education. Nations are spending up to 8 per cent of gross national product on education—and the proportion is rising. The growth of education gradually changes attitudes and tastes. The high quality of Swedish newspapers reveals a genuine and intelligent interest in politics among all classes of the Swedish people. In Britain a third of the adult population are members of at least some kind of political or professional organisation. Though this does not imply any deep political involvement, it does show an interest in the workings of society at all levels. The political apathy so noticeable among the affluent societies may, therefore, be just the first stage of the new society. There is, at least, a chance that apathy may be succeeded by informed, intelligent participation and criticism.

It is the task of Democratic Socialists to strengthen democratic institutions by encouraging participation at all levels. There must be institutional reform. Parliaments must be attuned to and competent to deal with the problems of affluence. This means that the best equipped of all sections of the community must be encouraged to enter parliament; and, once they get there, must have the facilities and opportunities to question government decisions. There must also be a genuine dialogue between parliament and the electorate. The individual member must know the problems of his constituents; the people as a whole must know what is going on in parliament. There should also be a strong second layer of democratic institutions—including local government and regional institutions, voluntary organisations like the trade unions, co-operatives and consumer groups, and meeting places for pressure groups like the central bargaining between trade unions and employers in Sweden.

Governments must enlarge the whole system of education. This does not only mean building more schools and universities; it also implies the provision of a whole network of educational facilities, including adult education, educational television, and an informed and lively mass-media. Only through such an educational system can there be mass-participation in democracy. In the affluent society, the mark of a strong democracy will not only be the participation of its people at all levels; it will also be the awareness and concern of its people for the problems of peoples in other countries.

8 International Relations

PRINCIPLES

Sceptics often deny that there can be an attitude towards other countries which is peculiarly Socialist. Foreign policy, they claim, is dictated by 'the national interest' and the facts of international power, and will be the same whichever party is in power.

The hard-headed realist's 'national interests' begs the question. In 1956 the British Conservative party and their Prime Minister, Sir Anthony Eden, believed that it was in 'the national interest' to attack the Egyptians at Suez. The British Labour Party, led by Hugh Gaitskell, argued that the Suez expedition was wrong, not because it was a disastrous failure, but because it was against 'the national interest'. The Conservatives assumed at Suez that it was in 'the national interest' to use force and establish a domination over another people, and that the only way to preserve British commercial enterprises was by use of force. To the Labour Party and other European Socialists, 'the national interest' is something much more complicated. The true interests of a nation are the standard of living, health, education of all its people. These interests are shared by other nations and can, in fact, only be promoted by common action. Aggression by one nation against another, like revolution in a democracy, is wrong.

Socialists believe the principles of freedom and equality cannot be fulfilled within a purely national context. Democratic Socialism does not just mean that every Englishman, German, or Nigerian is worthy of equal respect, but that every human being, irrespective of race, is worthy of equal respect.

Co-operation, not coercion, must therefore be the guiding principle of a Democratic Socialist foreign policy. In the words of the 1951 Frankfurt Declaration of the Socialist International, 'The new world society for which Socialists strive can develop fruitfully in peace only if it is based on voluntary co-operation between nations.'

In the nuclear age, a world order based on the domination of one nation over another or on warring national interests is unthinkable. In 1953 the British Labour statesman and Nobel Peace Prize winner, Philip Noel-Baker, wrote, 'International anarchy is a technological as well as a political and spiritual anachronism.' Thirteen years later his remark is even more relevant to a world which went close to the brink of a nuclear holocaust over Cuba in 1962. Today, every statesman—Democratic Socialist, Conservative or Communist—must think in terms of co-operation if the world is to survive. That is why Socialists support the United Nations and the rule of law. That is why they work for disarmament and the growth of world government through the strengthening of the United Nations.

Socialists, however, realise that until they reach the twin goals of world government and disarmament, a nation's security has to be maintained. It is still true that power counts for something in the world. The two major powers, the United States and Soviet Russia, are heard at the United Nations as much for their sheer size and power as for high principles or good ideas. In a world where there is no United Nations security force, nations still have to protect themselves by armaments and alliances.

The main architect of the North Atlantic Treaty Organisation of April 1949 was the British Labour Foreign Minister, Ernest Bevin. The N.A.T.O. alliance was supported by all Socialist parties of those countries that joined the alliance except the Italian Nenni Socialists. Acceptance of N.A.T.O. by Socialists was not a mass desertion of principle but an agreement to a defensive alliance to deter Russian territorial ambitions. After 1945, Socialists had hoped to continue their wartime friendship with Russia. But by 1948 Russia, under the imperialist Joseph Stalin, threatened to subject Western Europe to the same tyranny she had just imposed on Eastern Europe. A defensive alliance between Western Europe and the United States was one of the ways to stop Russia exploiting European war exhaustion.

Yet moral leadership can be just as influential as power. Sweden and Norway are negligible in terms of military power, but are very influential in world affairs, particularly at the United Nations. Democratic Socialists have always believed in the force of moral ideas. A Socialist Prime Minister of Belgium, Vandervelde, speaking in 1939 of the Labour Party's wholehearted support for the League of Nations, said, 'The Labour Party's stand for collective security has been the greatest moral fact in world affairs.' It might seem curious that three years after the virtual death of the League of Nations and a year before Hitler overran Belgium anybody should have supposed that moral ideas had any force at all. But Vandervelde was proved right by events. In 1945 the United Nations was created by the victorious Allies out of the ashes of the League —and now plays such an important part in world affairs that it is impossible to imagine a world without it. Yet the League of Nations or United Nations idea had not become practical politics until 1917—and after its creation was politely ignored by British Conservative politicians like Baldwin (who took his summer holiday every year near Geneva, the headquarters of the League, but never bothered to visit it). This growth in the popularity and influence of the United Nations was not the result of naked power but of moral force.

THE SOCIALIST INTERNATIONAL

The International was the first practical expression of the internationalism of Socialism. The First International, founded in 1864, broke up in sterile squabbling between Marxists and Anarchists. The Second International, set up in 1889, was a much more serious affair because it was an international of the rapidly growing mass Socialist parties rather than a meeting of warring and unrepresentative cliques. The International provided a forum at which all the national Socialist parties could thrash out the great problems of the day; whether a Socialist party should aim at revolution or at reform by parliamentary means; how Socialists could prevent wars. The International passed resolutions on these problems; and, when it was a question that concerned party discipline or the correct interpretation of Marxist doctrine, these resolutions were obeyed by the member parties.

The Second International also provided the Socialist parties with a ready-made foreign policy. In the words of the 1907 Stuttgart resolution, 'Wars are inherent in the nature of capitalism.' If war was the inevitable result of the rivalry between capitalists competing for overseas markets, there could be no conflict of interests between workers. The 1904 Amsterdam meeting of the International witnessed the spectacle of the Russian delegate, Plekhanov, and the Japanese delegate, Katayama, shaking hands while their two countries were at war—an impressive symbol of working-class unity. Each year the German Social Democrats voted against the army credits in the German Reichstag; and they voted, too, against the navy credits required by Tirpitz and the Kaiser for the construction of the Dreadnoughts. Though the International was almost exclusively European, it regularly condemned European imperialism—particularly British rule in India.

Despite all these excellent resolutions and intentions, the great European powers went to war in 1914. The importance of national ties among the Socialist parties had been illustrated long before the war when both Bebel, the German Social Democrat leader, and Jaurès, the French Socialist, had made it clear that a defensive war against a particular country was permissible—in Germany's case against Czarist Russia, and in France's case against Imperial Germany. The Socialist leaders hoped that the spread of Socialism and the existence of the Socialist International would ensure peace; but they could have stopped the war only if they had had complete control over their respective military machines. Tragically, war created a new patriotism amongst the working-classes; to retain their support most Socialists reluctantly supported the war. In the words of Ernest Bevin, 'I came to the conclusion that I would do my best to preserve the economic unity of the men I represent and accept passively the opinions of the majority of men.'[1] The fact remains, however, that the Socialists alone made a sustained effort to prevent war. The European statesmen and military planners merely blundered and stumbled into war. The Second International was important, too, as an early expression of internationalism in a world of empires and nation states. Indeed, the impetus behind the League of Nations owed much to its pioneering work.

In 1919 the Communists split the International and broke away to found the third or Communist International, based on Moscow. Some Socialist parties, including the Austrian Socialists, tried to bring the Communists and Socialists together in one International. But this attempt failed and, in 1923, a separate Labour and Socialist International was formed. After useful work, this International was undermined by the international crises of the 1930s. In 1951 a new Democratic Socialist International was formed at Frankfurt. Unlike its predecessors, this International has a large number of non-European Democratic Socialist parties affiliated to it; and plays an important part in co-ordinating the policies of Democratic Socialist parties of the world.

There are two main reasons why the International now plays only a co-ordinating role in the shaping of Socialist foreign policies. The first is that, in most Western democracies, Socialists are either the government or opposition, whereas the second International was primarily a substitute for a foreign policy for parties with little chance of immediate power. A Socialist government is forced to devise and carry out its own

1 Alan Bullock, *The Life and Times of Ernest Bevin.* Heinemann, 1960.

foreign policy. Inevitably each government stresses its individual approach to world problems. In the words of Harold Wilson, the Socialist International is now 'a meeting place of free independent national parties where leading Socialist statesmen meet regularly to thrash out their differences'. The second reason is that the International is now no longer the only international forum. The United Nations provides a meeting place not only for Socialists but for the statesmen of all the world. The hopes that were centred on the Second International have turned to the United Nations.

THE UNITED NATIONS

The establishment of the League of Nations in 1920 was a watershed in world politics. The League of Nations and its successor, the United Nations, constituted a rejection of the old court diplomacy and lawless power politics that had been the background to the 1914–18 war, and an attempt to put in their place an entirely new system of international relations. Thus, in the General Assembly, Councils and Commissions of the United Nations, common business is conducted by public debate. Under the United Nations' system, international relations are governed by the law of the Charter, the constitutions of the Agencies, and by numerous conventions on matters of common interest. In essence, the United Nations is an attempt to apply the principles of parliamentary democracy to international relations.

The key figure in promoting the idea of the League of Nations after the 1914–18 war was the Democratic President of the United States, Woodrow Wilson. After 1919, the work of setting up the covenant was supervised by Smuts, the South African statesman, and the independent-minded British Conservative, Lord Robert Cecil.[2] The statesmen were strongly backed by European public opinion. The peoples of Europe

2 *See* Philip Noel-Baker, 'The League of Nations' in *The Baldwin Age.* Eyre and Spottiswoode, 1960.

had suffered four years of modern warfare; and this experience had greatly discredited the old diplomacy that had led to them.

The British Labour Party played an important role in the establishment of the League. Some members of the Labour Party in Parliament, including the leader of the Parliamentary Party, Ramsay MacDonald, had voted against the British war effort. They and a number of dissident Liberals (most of whom later became members of the Labour Party), intellectuals, and members of the Fabian Society, worked out a plan for the establishment of a new supranational authority. Then, in 1917, when Arthur Henderson, the Labour leader, resigned from the War Cabinet, the Labour Party, together with the Trades Union Congress, produced a statement of war aims, which included the setting up of a League of Nations. When in January 1918 Lloyd George agreed to support Woodrow Wilson in establishing a permanent League of Nations (suggested by Woodrow Wilson in his address to the United States Congress of January 1918), one of the factors that contributed to his decision was the publication of Labour's war aims.

The principles of the League of Nations were drawn up in the covenant of the League signed at Versailles by the Peace Conference powers. Perhaps the most important single article of the covenant (certainly in President Wilson's opinion) was Article 10. This article was as follows: 'The members of the League undertake to respect and preserve as against external aggression the territorial integrity and existing political independence of all members of the League. In case of any such aggression, or in case of any threat or danger of such aggression, the Council shall advise upon the means by which this obligation shall be fulfilled.' Articles 11 to 16 laid down the procedure to be followed to safeguard peace. The League of Nations headquarters were set up at Geneva in Switzerland. With the single exception of the U.S.A., every then recognised state was at one period or another a member of the League of Nations.

Socialist governments gave the new world organisation full support. The Swedish Prime Minister, Branting, and, after his death, the Swedish Foreign Minister, Unden, were very active in upholding the authority of the League. Branting joined with Lord Robert Cecil and Nansen, the Norwegian statesman, in backing the authority of the League against Mussolini when he bombarded Corfu in 1923. Branting and Unden gave their full support to the plan to bring the dispute between Britain and Turkey, over the former Turkish province of Mosul, to the council of the League; and played a part in getting a settlement that was accepted by both sides. Unden and Vandervelde played a leading role in securing the admission of the defeated Germany to the council of the League in 1926.

Inevitably, however, the defence of the League's authority and the upholding of the idea of collective security depended on the great powers, which, given the fact that the United States and, up to 1934, Soviet Russia were not members, meant Britain and France. During the critical period in the history of the League, the French Socialist party was in opposition. In Britain, however, Ramsay MacDonald formed the two minority Labour governments of 1924 and 1929–31. Support of the League was the main plank in the foreign policy of both governments. Labour fought the 1923 General Election on a policy of international co-operation through a strengthened and enlarged League of Nations. MacDonald, who acted as his own Foreign Secretary in the 1923–24 government, sought to convince France that her long-term security against Germany could only come from a strengthened League of Nations. He did this by the Geneva Protocol of 1924 which combined the three principles of collective security, all-round disarmament and compulsory arbitration. However, a General Election brought the Conservatives to power and they promptly rejected the Protocol. In 1929 the Labour Party once again formed a government. The Labour Party's foreign policy was based on four principles; strengthening the League of Nations; international economic co-operation; compulsory arbitration; and disarmament. Arthur Henderson, the new Foreign Secretary, became the League's leading figure—and for two years the League became the arbiter of the world. Following Britain's initiative, more than forty countries signed the Optional Clause which provided for a system of compulsory arbitration under the Permanent Court of Justice. Henderson also persuaded the council of the League to organise a Disarmament Conference.

Tragically, the whole structure of the League was undermined by the world-wide economic crisis and by the revolutionary situation in Germany brought about by mass unemployment. In 1931 the slump destroyed the British Labour government and the Japanese invaded Manchuria. By 1933, the Disarmament Conference had failed. The League's last chance to reassert its authority came in 1935 when Mussolini invaded Abyssinia. The Socialist reaction was immediate. A joint conference of the General Council of the International Federation of Trade Unions and the Executive of the Labour and Socialist International called for 'prompt and effective sanctions' to put an end to the monstrous outrage upon international law, and assured the League of its whole-hearted support 'in the application of whatever sanctions may be necessary to stop this outrageous war and to restore peace'. The four Scandinavian powers—two of whom (Sweden and Norway) had Socialist governments—called for sanctions. The British Labour Party Annual Conference voted for sanctions against Mussolini, including military sanctions, by a majority of 95·2 per cent of the vote. The strong Labour line, together with the success of the Peace Ballot which had Labour support, forced the British Conservative government to uphold the authority of the League. But once the 1935 election was won the Conservative government changed its tune and condoned Italian aggression. This action, which was followed by concessions to German aggression, finished the League and destroyed any hope of peace.

Yet the work of those who had striven to make the League

of Nations a reality was not in vain. After the second World War, in October 1945, the United Nations was set up. This was a triumph for Socialist ideals. The Universal Declaration of the United Nations Charter itself affirms the equality of all men. The Labour Foreign Minister of Australia, Evatt, as President of the General Assembly of the United Nations, said that the Declaration had 'the authority of the body of opinion of the United Nations as a whole, and millions of men, women and children all over the world will turn for help, guidance and inspiration to this document'.

The principles of the charter are the same as those of the covenant of the League of Nations. In two ways, however, the United Nations is immeasurably stronger than the League. First, the two most powerful nations, the United States and Soviet Russia, in spite of their hostility to each other, are both members of the United Nations, whereas the United States in spite of her support for League activities had never been a member of the League, and Soviet Russia had only been so for a short time. Secondly, the United Nations is far more universal (except for the lamentable exclusion of China) than the League ever was. It has African and Asian as well as European and Latin American members. Indeed it is now impossible to get a majority in the General Assembly without the support of the Afro-Asian countries.

Socialists played a leading part in the establishment of the United Nations. Clement Attlee, as deputy Prime Minister in Churchill's war coalition government, was a member of the British delegation at the San Francisco Conference of 1945 which drew up the Charter. Australia, New Zealand, Norway and Sweden, all with Socialist governments, helped make the Charter, and led a middle power stand, though without success, against the grant of a veto to the permanent members of the Security Council of the United Nations. The first President of the General Assembly was the Belgian Socialist statesman, Paul Henri Spaak, while the first Secretary-General, Trygve Lie, was a Norwegian Socialist. The British Labour government of 1945–51 realised that in a nuclear world (the allies dropped atomic bombs on Hiroshima and Nagasaki in August 1945) it was essential that the United Nations should establish itself and grow in authority. Indeed, Ernest Bevin, when, as British Foreign Secretary, he opened the Executive Committee of the Preparatory Commission in August 1945, wondered what might be 'the effects of the atomic bomb on the organisation of security', and whether 'a great many of their previous conceptions and a great many of the assumptions on which they had worked at San Francisco would have to be radically revised'. President Truman of the United States, Mackenzie King of Canada, and the Labour Prime Minister, Clement Attlee, formally proposed a United Nations Commission on Atomic Energy to control the use of all nuclear power. Tragically, the growing hostility of Russia spoiled this chance of revolutionising international relations. The Russians made the proceedings of this Commission a farce. Indeed, the 'cold war' between the Communist bloc and the West threatened to undermine the structure of the United Nations. Russia used her veto in the Security Council as a way of weakening the United Nations.

Despite the 'cold war', and numerous crises, however, the success of the United Nations (now housed at Turtle Bay, New York) has been remarkable. The United Nations has been responsible for preventing or halting war in Persia, Greece, Kashmir, the Middle East from 1947 (including Suez), the Lebanon, West Irian and the Congo; and the Secretary-General of the United Nations, U Thant, played a contributory role in the solution of the Cuban crisis. In 1950, the United Nations did not stop Korea being invaded; but the invaders were resisted by a United Nations army composed of the troops of seventeen member nations with the express approval of the vast majority of the rest, including India. Its various specialist organisations (whose establishment was originally opposed by Soviet Russia) have earned the United Nations international prestige; the World Health Organisation in public health matters; the International Labour Organisation in improving labour conditions; the Food and Agricultural Organisation in pioneering agricultural research and development; the United Nations Educational, Scientific, and Cultural Organisation in promoting education and research; the International Bank for reconstruction and development (financed by members' subscriptions) in loaning funds for economic development; and the International Monetary Fund (also financed by members' subscriptions) which promotes international trade and exchange stability by making needed currencies available to members and by financing technical assistance.

Socialist support for the United Nations has been impressive. In 1951 the Frankfurt Declaration of the Socialist International said, 'Democratic Socialism regards the establishment of the United Nations as an important step towards an international community.' Eleven years later the Oslo declaration of the Socialist International said, 'The Charter of the United Nations and the decisions based on it should be accepted by all.'

The British Labour Party, in power or in opposition, has upheld the authority of the United Nations, perhaps most impressively over the Suez crisis of 1956 when the United Nations General Assembly declared that Britain, France and Israel, in invading Egyptian territory, were acting in violation of their Charter pledges. Norway and Sweden have been leading members of those small group of middle sized countries (which include Canada, Iceland, Tunisia, Nigeria and Yugoslavia) who are known as the 'fire brigade' countries. These countries have taken the initiative in appropriating to the General Assembly those peace-making powers which were meant to belong to the Security Council alone; and have worked with the Secretary-General (particularly the Swede, Hammarskjöld, and after his death, U Thant) in helping to preserve world peace—in Egypt in 1956, in the Congo in 1960 where United Nations' troops prevented Africa from becoming a football in the 'cold war', in West Irian in 1962, and in the Yemen in 1963.

Socialists, however, believe that the aim of their policy should be so to strengthen the powers of the United Nations that it becomes the nucleus of world government. The Socialist parties of the European Economic Community (set up by the Treaty of Rome in 1956) see European unity as another step towards world government. All Socialist parties, however, agree on the crucial role of the United Nations. The Oslo Declaration of the Socialist International says, 'The ultimate objective of the parties of the Socialist International is nothing less than world government. As a first step towards it, they seek to strengthen the United Nations so that it may become more and more effective as an instrument for maintaining peace.' Hugh Gaitskell, then leader of the British Labour Party, put forward an eight-point programme for strengthening the United Nations in October 1962, shortly before his death. Among the points he proposed were: the establishment of the nucleus of a permanent international police force; the setting up of a disarmament agency to secure and supervise a disarmament agreement; the admission of Communist China to the United Nations; and the reformation of the Security Council and the Economic and Social Council to make them more representative of the countries of Asia and Africa.

DISARMAMENT

Philip Noel-Baker has said, 'Disarmament is the preliminary, indispensable condition of world government. Until disarmament is achieved, world government, stable peace and the rule of law will remain a promising, but a precarious hope.'

Socialists have always advocated disarmament. For they believe that the arms race, to which the competition in the invention and production of arms inevitably leads, is one of the main causes of war. Before the 1914–18 war the Second International called for general disarmament. After the first World War, the British Labour governments of 1923–24 and 1929–31 took the initiative in trying to secure general disarmament. The abortive Geneva Protocol of 1924, the brain-child of Arthur Henderson, was based on disarmament. Ramsay MacDonald was primarily responsible in getting agreement on naval disarmament by the London Treaty of 1930 between Britain, the United States and Japan. But the most important disarmament negotiations of all before the Second World War was the Disarmament Conference of 1932–1934. The ground for this conference was prepared by Arthur Henderson, Labour's Foreign Secretary. Though by the time the Disarmament Conference had begun, Labour had been dismissed from office, Henderson became the Conference's chairman. The conference began in inauspicious circumstances; the world was over-shadowed by economic crisis; early in 1932 the Japanese militarists had invaded Manchuria. Yet, in the view of Philip Noel-Baker, the turning point was the rejection by the British National government (dominated by the Conservatives) of the Hoover plan for all-round armament reduction.

The need for disarmament in the modern world of nuclear weapons is even greater. President Kennedy said to the United Nations General Assembly, 'Today every inhabitant of this planet must contemplate the day when it may no longer be habitable. Every man, woman and child lives under a nuclear sword of Damocles, hanging by the slenderest of threads, capable of being cut at any moment by accident, miscalculation or madness.' The arms race daily threatens the world with accidental war; and by its presence provokes international crises. The American U2 aircraft, which was sent by President Eisenhower over Russia as part of America's defence against Russian surprise attack, destroyed the Paris Summit meeting of May 1960. The United States Secretary of State, Dean Rusk, has described the Cuban crisis of October 1962 as 'an arms race crisis'.

Since 1945, Socialists have continuously supported disarmament. In 1962 the Oslo Declaration of the Social International said, 'The Socialist International stands for complete disarmament both in nuclear and conventional weapons, including all and subject to truly effective controls.' It was the British Labour government of 1945–51 which put disarmament on the map. The failure of the joint proposals of Clement Attlee, together with Truman and King, to set up a United Nations Commission on Atomic Energy, has been described above. Every year from 1945–51 the British delegation to the United Nations presented annual resolutions in favour of total disarmament and the setting up of a Disarmament Commission to prepare proposals for a draft treaty. In 1952 the United Nations Disarmament Commission was set up (which combined the function of the Commission on Atomic Energy and the Commission on Conventional Armaments). Sweden has played a prominent part in the work of the United Nations Disarmament Committee of eighteen which is trying to get Russia, Britain and the United States to agree to a Disarmament Treaty. Individual Socialists, including Jules Moch, former French Socialist Prime Minister, Minister of the Interior, and Minister of Defence and French delegate to the United Nations Disarmament Committee, and Philip Noel-Baker, have made important contributions to the cause of disarmament.

The key signatures, however, to any Disarmament Treaty must be Soviet Russia, France, the United States, Great Britain and Communist China. Disarmament negotiations between these powers have dragged on through the 1950s and early 1960s with little result. It is here that Great Britain, and the British Labour government, has a crucial part to play. The difference between the American and Russian negotiation positions is comparatively small. A determined Labour government, committed to disarmament, might possibly achieve a significant break-through in disarmament negotiations. If a disarmament treaty were signed, this would be a crucial step towards world government. It would also release resources that could be used for other purposes—including aid for the underdeveloped countries. In the words of Harold Wilson, 'the future of mankind depends on achieving a breakthrough at the conference table'.

9 The Developing World

The first seven chapters have shown how European Democratic Socialism was almost entirely the product of a post-industrial society. The peoples of the emergent countries of Africa, Asia, and Latin America have had to develop institutions in very different circumstances. This last chapter describes the interaction between Socialism and democracy in the imperialist countries and the nationalism of the colonial peoples, analyses briefly the problems of the 'new' nations, and examines ways in which European Socialists can help them.

THE END OF EMPIRE

In 1914 Europe dominated the world. Most European nations had empires outside Europe: the British Empire was the largest and included India, Ceylon, Burma and Malaya in Asia, large chunks of Africa, and the 'white' self-governing territories of Canada, Australia and New Zealand. Indo-China in Asia, and much of North and West Africa belonged to France: Holland ruled the islands of the East Indies (now called Indonesia): Russia had extended her rule in Central Asia over the principalities of Turkistan; Germany ruled over Tanganyika in East Africa, the Cameroons, and Togo in West Africa, and South West Africa; Portugal had colonies in Angola and Mozambique; Italy had carved out an empire in the Horn of Africa; even Belgium had ruthlessly acquired for herself the vast and valuable territory in the Congo. European industrial might triumphed over the pre-industrial societies of the rest of the world. But by 1965 European colonialism was almost dead.

Socialists played a leading role in the destruction of the colonial system. Because they believed in equality, they rejected even the most enlightened imperialism as at bottom little more than the domination by force of one people over another. They agreed with J. A. Hobson, when he wrote, 'Imperialism is a depraved choice of national life, imposed by self-seeking interests which appeal to the lusts of quantitative acquisitiveness and of forceful domination surviving in a nation from early centuries of animal struggle for existence.'

From the first they opposed acts of imperialism. The Second International condemned the European 'scramble for Africa' in strong terms and, with other humanitarians, they denounced the atrocities that characterised the personal rule of the Belgian king, Leopold II, in the Congo. The French and German Socialists both campaigned vigorously against their government's aggressive Moroccan policies. Socialists opposed the Boer War (1899–1902) between Britain and the Boers in South Africa. Ramsay MacDonald, one of the leading members of the infant Labour Party, wrote about British rule in India, 'India's peace . . . has been at the price of her own initiative. That is the real objection to all attempts to govern a country by a benevolent imperialism.'

In his work *Imperialism: the last stage of capitalism*, written in 1917, Lenin tried to explain why the developments in capitalist society that Marx had foreseen had not, in fact, taken place. He blamed imperialism; but argued that imperialism, as the last stage in capitalism, contained the seeds of violent revolution. He said, 'Imperialism is capitalism in that stage of development in which the dominance of monopolies and finance capitalism has established itself; in which the export of capital has acquired pronounced importance; in which the division of the world among the international trusts has begun; in which the division of the globe amongst the great capitalist powers has been completed.' Lenin, then, gave the final twist to his theory by his prediction that imperialism could only lead to war and revolution. According to Lenin's theory of 'uneven development', capitalist powers develop unevenly. Eventually the situation will be reached when the newer capitalist powers will challenge the older established powers for their share of empire. Periodic world wars, Lenin concluded, must therefore be characteristic of imperialism, and the outbreak of war would be the signal for the revolt of the colonial peoples against exploitation by their imperialist masters—and the revolt of the workers of the imperialist countries against exploitation by the capitalists. The crucial flaw in Lenin's *Imperialism*, as in Marx's *Capital*, was his failure to take into account the consequences of democracy and the rise of Democratic Socialism.

Since the British Empire was the largest empire and India the largest colony, the role of the British Labour Party in the liquidation of imperialism was obviously crucial. By 1918 the Labour Party was committed to Indian independence. But between 1918 and 1939, because it was in power only for two short periods on a minority basis, it was unable to take any decisive action. In any case, as Clement Attlee, then leader of the Labour Party, wrote: 'Whatever may have been the history of the acquisition of the British Colonial Empire, the fact remains that Great Britain is responsible for the welfare of millions of coloured people. It is not possible simply to relinquish control, for the impact of European civilisation has been felt by all native communities, generally with a disintegrating effect upon the structure of society.' During the inter-war period, therefore, the emphasis of Labour Party policy was on improving the conditions of imperialist rule and preparing the colonies for independence.

The two crucial factors in Indian independence—the beginning of the end of the imperialist system—were the strength of the Indian Congress Party under Gandhi, Nehru and Patel and the courage of Attlee's Labour administration. The 1939–1945 war greatly strengthened the nationalist movements in the colonial territories. The spread of education, the beginnings of a market economy, and the growth in mass media of communications, resulted in the emergence of mass political movements in Asia and parts of Africa, pledged to independence. In Asia, Japanese victories over European nations also had a considerable impact. On 14 August 1941, President Roosevelt and Prime Minister Churchill declared in the Atlantic Charter (against the wishes of the Conservative leader Churchill, who hoped to make the British Empire an exception), 'they respect the right of all peoples to choose the form of government under which they will live.' This was taken up by nationalist leaders everywhere as a peg on which to hang their claims. By 1943 the coalition government of Churchill had been forced by the war to go some of the way towards meeting the Indian Congress leaders' demands.

Returned to power with a huge majority in 1945, the Attlee government, in spite of Conservative opposition, committed itself to early Indian independence. On the departure of the Cabinet Mission to India in 1946, Attlee said, 'India herself must choose what will be her future constitution: what will be her position in the world.' He also said in 1946, 'we do not desire to retain within the Commonwealth and Empire any unwilling peoples.' By the end of 1947, India, Pakistan and Ceylon had become independent. In 1948, Burma followed suit. By this conscious and imaginative act of policy, 450 million people were freed from colonial rule. A great tribute to Labour Party policy was paid when all these nations, except Burma, remained within the Commonwealth as independent nations.

Meanwhile, the Attlee administration prepared the rest of Britain's colonies (mostly in Africa) for independence. In the words of the 1948 White Paper, 'The central purpose of British colonial policy is simple. It is to guide the colonial territories to responsible self-government within the Commonwealth in conditions that ensure to the peoples concerned both a fair standard of living and freedom from oppression in any quarter.' As a logical extension of regarding the interests of the colonial peoples as paramount, the Labour government developed the planned expansion of the economies of the colonial territories which had begun under the wartime coalition. When Labour came into office, it asked each colony to prepare a ten-year development plan to provide a framework for the future economic structure—the roads, irrigation, social services and soil conservation. Two public corporations were set up—the Colonial Development Corporation and the Overseas Development Corporation—to provide colonial economic enterprises. In addition, a big educational programme was begun to train the colonial peoples for administration.

The policies of the Labour government could not be reversed by their successors, the Conservatives. It is true that Conservative cabinets were responsible for two bloody colonial revolts in Kenya and Cyprus. But after 1959 Macmillan's Conservative government, with full Labour support, granted independence to most of the remaining colonies in Africa. France, with the next largest Empire, managed the retreat from imperialism far less well. She fought full-scale, senseless and costly wars in Indo-China and Algeria. The Algerian war destroyed the Fourth Republic. The French Socialists have little to be proud of in their record in colonial affairs. Despite Gaston Defferre's liberal policy as Minister responsible for French Africa, Guy Mollet's Socialist-led Coalition Government of 1956–57 must go down in history as the government that gave way to the French settlers in Algeria. In the end, however, France, Holland and Belgium were all forced by the pressure of the independence movements to dissolve their empires. There are no major colonies left in Asia. In 1965 only Southern Rhodesia, the Portuguese colonies, and South Africa remained as the last relics of the 'scramble for Africa'. European political imperialism is nearly dead.

UNDERDEVELOPMENT

The central fact about the world, despite pockets of affluence, is still its poverty. Imperialism has left the former colonies poor. One can argue that if these countries had never been brought under Western rule they would be even poorer. It is true that the British brought law and order to India and Africa, without which there can be no sustained economic expansion; and, in India, built the railways, canals and roads which are part of the 'infra-structure' of a modern economy. Yet British officials did little to encourage Indian and African economic activities; and their economies remained subservient and geared to the British economy. This attitude was changed only by the advent of Labour to power in Britain in 1945—but by that time India was on the eve of independence and it was Africa (formerly cruelly neglected) that became the chief beneficiary of this new policy. Whatever the effects of colonialism, between one-third and one-half of mankind are still under-nourished. Two-thirds of the peoples of the world are still hopelessly poor. There is a fantastic difference in wealth between the under-developed and the industrialised countries. At one extreme, North Americans enjoy an annual income of about £700 for every man, woman and child. At the other extreme, the comparative figure for the two-thirds of mankind who live in underdeveloped countries is £30. It has been calculated that in 1800 Britain, France, Germany and the United States enjoyed per capita incomes several times as high as most of the underdeveloped countries enjoy now.[1]

The difference in wealth between the industrialised countries of the West and the 'underdeveloped' countries is actually increasing. During the 1950s the rate of increase in income per capita in the 'underdeveloped' countries was on average only 1 per cent per annum (barely keeping up with their unprecedented increase in population); while the annual per capita income increase in the industrialised countries was 2½ per cent (some European countries, for example Western Germany, France, Italy and Sweden, advanced much faster than this). The Swedish economist and Socialist thinker, Professor

1 S. Kuznets, *Underdeveloped Countries and the Pre-industrial Phase in the Advanced Countries,* United Nations, World Population Conference, 1954.

Myrdal, has pointed out that 'the play of the forces of the market normally tends to increase, rather than to decrease, the inequalities....' Marx's prophecy of increasing inequality, which has been falsified for *internal* class divisions in Western Europe, has thus been unexpectedly realised in the field of *external* national divisions.

'Underdevelopment' is not, however, just an economic term. It also describes a social state as well. In many underdeveloped countries the machinery of administration and law is inadequate for the building of a modern nation. Their peoples are often culturally and socially divided and only the accidents of history and a common desire for independence unite them. There is a high percentage of illiteracy. While the task of European Socialist governments was to control and share out the fruits of an already industrialised economy, the governments of many of the emergent nations have not only to create an industrialised economy but also to build up and hold together an enduring national structure.

SOCIALISM AND NATION-BUILDING

Many of the leaders of the emergent countries believe in Socialism. In Asia, Jawaharlal Nehru, first Prime Minister of India, was a fervent Socialist—and since 1954 the ruling Indian Congress Party has been committed to the establishment of 'a Socialist pattern of society'. The great majority of Asian political leaders are committed to Socialism in some form. African political leaders have laid particular stress on 'African Socialism'. Jomo Kenyatta, President of one of the most recently independent countries, Kenya, introduced the manifesto of the Kenya African National Union with these words, 'Our achievement of independence, for which we have struggled so long, will not be an end in itself. It will give us the opportunity to work unfettered for the creation of a Democratic African Socialist Kenya.' Julius Nyerere, President of Tanzania, said, 'Ujamaa, then, or "familyhood", describes our Socialism. It is opposed to capitalism, which seeks

to build a happy society on the basis of the exploitation of man
by man. And it is equally opposed to doctrinaire Socialism,
which seeks to build its happy society on a philosophy of inevitable conflict between man and man.' When President
Senghor of Senegal spoke at the Dakar Conference of Decem-
ber 1962 on 'African roads to Socialism', he said, 'Socialism is
the merciless fight against social dishonesties and injustices;
fraudulent conversion of public funds, rackets and bribes. ...'

The adoption by African political leaders of their own
brand of Socialism raises the question of how relevant the
institutions of European Socialism are to the problems of the
underdeveloped countries. The leaders of the underdeveloped
nations speak in terms of Socialist ideals. This is partly because
the first generation of nationalist leaders has always had
closer contacts with European Socialists than with any other
body of opinion. Nehru, Nyerere and Lee Kuan Yew learnt
their Socialism in England; Sekou Touré and Senghor learnt
theirs in France. More important, equality and freedom were
the basic arguments against imperialism; and they remain the
basic arguments against poverty, ignorance and disease.

It is clear, however, that the institutional framework of European Socialism does not, without considerable modification,
provide a model for the leaders of the developing countries.
India, it is true, has introduced and retained many of the
institutions characteristic of European democracy and European Socialism. But she started independence with an adequate administration and a leadership committed to and well-
versed in the running of Western institutions, and, despite the
poverty of her people, is at a later stage of development than
many other developing countries. The fact is that the developing countries face a different set of problems from those of the
industrialised countries. It is not surprising, therefore, that
they are creating institutions of their own to meet the particular circumstances of their societies.

Imperialist countries usually transferred power to elected
legislatures and usually left behind all the democratic institu-

tions—the independent judiciary, free Press, party system, independent trade unions and co-operatives—so characteristic of European democracy. This was in accordance with the stated wishes of the nationalist leaders who claimed power and independence in the name of democracy and freedom. Yet few of the underdeveloped countries except, perhaps, India, still retain all these democratic institutions. In most countries there has been a dramatic increase in the powers of the head of the executive—and a corresponding decline in the power of the elected legislatures. In Africa, one-party or military régimes are the norm. Examples of the former are Tanzania and most of the French-speaking states; of the latter, Ghana and Nigeria. In many states opposition parties have been banned or do not exist. In Asia, military leaders, as in Burma and Pakistan, have seized power from the political leaders.

The reasons for this abandonment of the Western parliamentary model by the developing countries stem from the fact of 'underdevelopment'. In most African and Asian states the first priority is to create a national consensus. There are many forces, in particular those of tribe, language, and culture, pulling the new nations apart. The chaos in the Congo since 1960 is a warning of what happens if these forces are let loose. The danger is that in these conditions Western parliamentary democracy would only add to the divisive forces. In Ghana, for example, some opposition leaders saw parliament as a springboard for dividing the nation on tribal lines rather than a platform for expressing legitimate grievances. It is not surprising, therefore, that Asian and African leaders have concentrated on building up executive power at the expense of parliamentary institutions.

The fact that the 'new' nations are committed to development is a further inducement to abandon the Western democratic model. It is argued first that, where talent is scarce, it is foolish to have part of the leading élite *hors de combat* in opposition. Secondly, development creates new tensions of its own. Some citizens expect poverty to be abolished overnight and are puzzled and resentful when this does not happen. Trade unionists often do not understand that the needs of the country demand that most of the increase in national wealth, instead of being immediately shared out in higher living standards, has to be reinvested to stimulate self-sustaining economic growth. Thirdly, and most important of all, the only way to stimulate a stagnant backward economy into self-perpetuating growth is by government initiative. Mr Nehru, in his last message to the Indian National Congress, said, 'It is inevitable that the major methods of production should be owned or controlled by the State. Otherwise the old order which we wish to change will continue and all vested interests of that order will flourish.' Indeed, for most statesmen of the developing countries the planning by the state of the development of the country's resources is the central part of Socialism. Once again the need for planning increases the power of the executive.

If, however, there are arguments for strong executive power, there are also arguments for there being continuous dialogue between the leaders and the peoples of developing countries. The Russian failure in the vital sector of agriculture has shown how lack of communication and resistance by the leaders to the opinions of the people can hold back development. The decline of Ghana's economy under Nkrumah illustrates what happens when the interests of the leadership are put before the interests of the people. The task of the leaders of backward countries must be to develop institutions that can secure this two-way flow of ideas. Only they can prevent their governments from becoming a self-perpetuating *élite*. Only they can ensure that they use their power to revolutionise the social and economic structure of their societies—and thus stimulate the transformation into a modern pluralist state.

THE ROLE OF DEMOCRATIC SOCIALISM

European Socialists must not expect miracles. They must remember, as J. P. Narayan has pointed out, that historically their own democracies were the product of industrialisation. They must realise, too, how fragile these still are. In any case their role is not that of judge. It is far more constructive— namely, to maintain close contacts with the developing world and to stimulate interest in the developing countries within their own societies. Their function must be to act as a gadfly to the consciences of the industrialised nations—particularly in the increase of technical and financial aid.

Just as Socialists have successfully used the political economic and social machinery of a single country to put right internal injustices, so there must be created and used international political economic and social machinery to help put right this world injustice. Harold Wilson said, 'He is no true Socialist if his faith stops dead at the shores of his native land'; and the 1962 Oslo Declaration of the Socialist International stated, 'It should be the consistent policy of the Socialist International to unite the Socialist forces of all countries in the great endeavour of accelerating the progress of the new States.'

Socialists realise that the industrialised countries must channel both financial and technical aid to the underdeveloped countries if their peoples are to stimulate quickly the development in industry and agriculture which alone can break the vicious circle of poverty. The Rome Declaration of the Socialist International of October 1961 declared that government aid by the industrialised to the underdeveloped countries should be increased to the equivalent of at least one per cent of their national income.

It is not just a question, however, of the amount of aid. Indeed, thanks to the enlightened policies of successive American presidents, the amount of aid channelled to the underdeveloped countries since the end of the war has been, on paper, quite impressive. In 1961 the total contribution of all Western countries amounted to £2,100 million. Unfortunately there have been serious deficiencies in the way in which aid is given and administered. Private investment can never be a substitute for public aid. Too much public aid, however, has been given in the form of short, high interest loans, with the result that the number of recipients of this aid whose debt has risen beyond the safety limit of ten per cent of exports has dramatically increased. Too often political factors have shaped policy. For example, almost one third of all United States aid has gone to three American 'ward' countries in Asia—South Korea, Formosa, and South Vietnam; while Soviet Russia has used aid as a foreign policy weapon. Its administration has been largely unplanned; and while Socialists support the principle of aid given on a non-political multilateral basis, there has been far too much overlapping in the work of the different United Nations agencies.

Socialists are well aware of the difficulties and have put forward suggestions for improvements in the machinery of international aid. The British Labour Party has called for the establishment of a World Development Agency to co-ordinate aid policies. In 1961, the Socialist International urged that aid should be given either as a gift or on a long-term loan basis rather than in the form of expensive short-term loans. The British Labour government argued in favour of regional planning if aid is to be used wisely by the underdeveloped countries. They point to the pioneer work in this field carried out by the British Labour government when it launched the Colombo Plan in 1950. The principle behind the plan is the co-ordination and supervision of aid and technical co-operation from Commonwealth countries to countries in South East Asia.

The Rome Declaration of the Socialist International stressed that trade was quite as important to the economic development of the poorer countries as aid. The industrialised countries must be prepared to buy the goods (including manufactured goods) produced by the underdeveloped countries. This implies a number of basic reforms in the world economy. Harold Wilson has advocated a change in the international liquidity situation. At present, the British and the United

States governments are forced to put a ceiling on trade (and aid as well) because of balance of payments difficulties. But one country's balance of payments deficit is another country's surplus. If the rich industrialised countries could be persuaded to increase international liquidity through a reformed International Monetary Fund, as suggested by Harold Wilson, then both trade and aid could be protected from balance of payments crises. There must also be reforms in the international tariff system to protect the new industries of the underdeveloped countries. Short-term fluctuations in prices of primary goods (on which the underdeveloped countries depend for export revenue) must be levelled out; in the short term, perhaps, by a fund to provide loans to offset cyclical fluctuations, such as France operates for the benefit of developing countries within the franc zone; in the long term by international price stabilisation agreements for all commodities.

Socialists in the West, who played a major part in raising the living standard of their own peoples, must now lead a crusade within their countries against world poverty. It will be a difficult task: for there is a strong tendency for the affluent societies to look inwards. Yet how can the peoples of the West in conscience enjoy an isolated affluence if the rest of the world remains in poverty?

Appendix

Chronological tables of the main Socialist parties and governments

AUSTRALIA

1891	AUSTRALIAN LABOUR PARTY (ALP) founded.
1904	Watson minority government.
1908–09	Fisher minority government.
1910–13 and 1914–16	Majority governments under Fisher and Hughes: pensions for invalids and maternity allowances; land taxes: established Commonwealth Bank.
1916	Party split on conscription.
1929–32	Scullin government. Party split.
1941–45	Curtin government.
1945–49	Forde, later Chifley, government; Social Services Consolidation Act; creation of public industries.
1955	Party split—formation of a mainly Catholic Democratic Labour Party.
1961	Defeated in General Election by one seat.

1963 Elections: 52 of 122 seats in Federal Parliament. 2,322,240 = 44·66 per cent of votes.

AUSTRIA

1889	Sozialdemokratische Partei Öesterreichs founded—name changed to SOZIALISTISCHE PARTEI ÖESTERREICHS (SPÖ) in 1945.
1914	87 seats in Reichsrat of Habsburg Monarchy.
1918	Austrian Republic founded: Socialist Renner first Chancellor.

1919–20   SPÖ—Christian Social Coalition.
1920   SPÖ goes into opposition.
1930   Largest party—72 seats out of 165.
1934   Banned by Dollfuss.
1945   Renner again Chancellor.
1945–66   SPÖ participates in 'permanent' coalition with People's Party: social security measures and nationalisation of key industries. Presidency and control over nationalised industries goes to Socialists. From 1959–65 Foreign Ministry held by Socialist Kreisky.
1966   SPÖ goes into opposition after People's Party election victory.

1966 Elections: 74 out of 165 seats in the Nationalrat. 1,928,922 votes = 42·6 per cent of votes.

FRANCE

1896   Different Socialist groups united briefly.
1905   SECTION FRANÇAISE DE L'INTERNATIONALE OUVRIÈRE (SFIO) founded.
1914   76 seats (1,106,000 votes). Guesde joins cabinet.
1920   Party split at Tours—Communist Party formed.
1936–37   Blum's Popular Front government; family allowances; 40 hour week; nationalisation of railways.
1944   Resistance Charter.
1944–46   All-party Provisional governments: Social Security Act; nationalisation of basic industries; Commissariat Général du Plan.
1946–47   Short-lived Socialist Blum government.
1947–51   SFIO partners in coalition governments.
1956–57   Mollet coalition government.
1957–58   SFIO partners in Coalition government and de Gaulle's first government.
1966   François Mitterand, left-wing candidate supported by SFIO, gets 45·5 per cent of vote on second Presidential ballot.

GERMANY

1863	General Workers' Association founded, leading to
1875	SOZIALDEMOKRATISCHE PARTIE DEUTSCHLANDS (SPD)
1878–90	Party declared illegal by Bismarck.
1890	35 seats (1,427,298 votes).
1891	Erfurt Programme.
1914	110 seats (4,250,329 votes) strongest party.
1919	Foundation of Weimar Republic: Socialists Ebert and Scheidemann, President and Chancellor, respectively.
1919–30	Weimar coalitions (SPD in 7 out of 15).
1930	Fall of Müller's SPD-led coalition marks end of parliamentary democracy.
1933	SPD banned by Hitler.
1933–45	Party leaders in prison or exile.
1949–	Main opposition party in Western German Republic: controls or participates in many state and municipal governments, including Berlin.

1965 Elections: 202 out of 496 seats in Bundestag. 12,813,185 = 39·3 per cent of votes.

ISRAEL

1909	First Kibbutz started at Degania in Palestine under Turkish rule.
1920	Foundation of Histadruth.
1922	British mandate over Palestine set up.
1930	Mapai, Israeli Labour party, founded.
1948	Creation of State of Israel.
1948	Mapam, left-wing Socialist party, founded.
1948–53	Ben Gurion Mapai-led coalition governments.
1953–55	Moshe Sharett Mapai-led coalition government.
1954	Mapam splits. Formation of Ahdut Ha'avoda.
1955–63	Ben Gurion Mapai-led coalition governments.
1963–	Eshkol Mapai-led coalition government. At 1965 general election Mapai presents a joint list of candidates with Ahdut Ha'avoda.

1965 Elections: Mapai–Ahdut Ha'avoda 45 out
of 120 seats in Knesset. 443,379
votes = 36·74 per cent of votes.

ITALY

1892	PARTITO SOCIALISTA ITALIANO (PSI) founded.
1913	53 seats.
1919	156 seats—largest single party.
1921	Leghorn Congress: party split, minority formed Communist Party.
1922	Further split into majority Socialists and Italian Workers' Socialist Party.
1926	Socialist parties suppressed by Mussolini.
1930	Majority Socialists and Italian Workers' Socialist Party unite in exile.
1943–47	Socialist participation in coalition governments.
1946	115 Socialists returned: second largest party.
1947	Split into Socialist Party (PSI) under Nenni and Social Democrats under Saragat (PSDI)
1962–	Centre Left Coalitions: PSDI participated from beginning, PSI joined in 1963—left wing splits off to form Socialist Party of Proletarian Unity.
1964	Saragat elected first Socialist President.
1966	PSI and PSDI reunite.

NEW ZEALAND

1890–1910	Strong Labour influence on Liberal governments.
1904	Political Labour League founded, followed by first Labour Party (1910), and United Labour Party (1913).
1913	Party split.
1914	Four seats.

1916	NEW ZEALAND LABOUR PARTY founded.
1925	Chief opposition party.
1935–40	Savage Government.
	Social Security Act: public works and
	nationalisation of Revenue Bank.
1940–49	Frazer Governments: further social security
	advances and nationalisation measures.
1957–60	Nash government.

1963 Elections: 35 out of 80 seats in Parliament. 524,073 votes = 43·76 per cent of votes.

NORWAY

1887	ARBEIDERPARTIET founded.
1903	First members in Storting.
1912	Party split.
1914	23 seats in Storting.
1923	Party split.
1927	Party reunited: largest in Storting with 59 seats.
1928	Government of few days only.
1935–39	Nygaardsvold government (with co-operation of Agrarians); Pensions Act; Insurance Act.
1939–45	Wartime coalition (in exile 1940–45 after German invasion).
1945–65	Gerhardson (1951–55 Torp) governments (apart from 28 days in 1963). Further social security advances; nationalisation of basic industries; planning system set up.
1965	After election defeat, Arbeiderpartiet goes into opposition, but remains by far the largest single party.

1965 Elections: 68 out of 150 seats in Storting. 879,036 votes = 46·3 per cent of votes.

SWEDEN

1889	SOCIALDEMOKRATISKA ARBETAR-PARTIET founded.
1896	Branting first Socialist in Riksdag.
1915	87 seats in Second House—largest single party.
1917–20	Social Democrats form a Coalition government with Liberals which introduces universal suffrage and responsible government.
1920 and 1921–23	Branting minority governments.
1924–26	Branting–Sandler minority governments.
1932–39	Hansson government with Agrarian support (except for short period in 1936: unemployment programme, including public works and social security measures.
1939–45	Hansson heads wartime coalition.
1945–46	Hansson government followed by
from 1946–	Successive Erlander governments, sometimes in coalition with Agrarians; further social security advances, including 1960 Old Age Pensions Act; housing and educational programmes.
	1964 Elections: 113 out of 223 seats in Lower House.
	2,006,921 votes=47·3 per cent of votes.

UNITED KINGDOM

1899	Two Independent Labour Party M.P.s and 13 Lib-Lab.
1900	Labour Representation Committee founded—name changed to LABOUR PARTY 1906.
1914	42 M.P.s.
1916	Henderson in War Cabinet.
1922	142 M.P.s main opposition party.
1924	MacDonald minority government
1929–31	MacDonald minority government.
1931	Labour government resigns: MacDonald and a few followers participate in Conservative-dominated 'National' government.

1940–45　Labour in wartime coalition government under Churchill with Attlee as Deputy Prime Minister (1942) and other Labour Ministers in War Cabinet.

1945–51　Atlee governments. National Health and National Insurance Acts; nationalisation of key industries; independence of India, Pakistan, Ceylon, and Burma.

1964–　Wilson governments: First National Plan, beginning of prices and incomes policy, introduction of comprehensive secondary education.

1966 Elections: 363 out of 629 seats in Parliament. 13,064,951 votes = 47·9 per cent of votes.

Short Bibliography

General

CAUTE, DAVID. *The Left in Europe Since 1789.* New York: Mc-Graw-Hill, 1966.

COLE, G. D. H. *A History of Socialist Thought.* 7 vols. London: Macmillan, 1953–60.

CROSLAND, C. A. R. *The Future of Socialism.* New York: Schocken Books, 1963.

LANDAUER, CARL. *European Socialism.* 2 vols. Berkeley: University of California, 1959.

Chapter 1

BRAATOY, BJARNE. *The New Sweden: A Vindication of Democracy.* Edinburgh: Thomas Nelson, 1939.

COLE, MARGARET. *Robert Owen of New Lanark.* London: Batchworth Press, 1953.

GAY, PETER. *The Dilemma of Democratic Socialism.* New York: Collier Books, 1962.

JACKSON, J. HAMPDEN. *Jean Jaurès.* London: Allen & Unwin, 1943.

LEE, JOHN A. *Socialism in New Zealand.* London: T. Werner Laurie, 1938.

PELLING, HENRY. *A Short History of the Labour Party.* New York: St. Martin's Press, 1961.

PLAMENATZ, J. P. *German Marxism and Russian Communism.* New York: Harper & Row, 1964.

ROSTOW, W. W. *The Stages of Economic Growth.* Cambridge: Cambridge University Press, 1961.

Chapter 2

ATLEE, CLEMENT. *The Labour Party in Perspective.* London: Victor Gollancz, 1937.

BEVAN, ANEURIN. *In Place of Fear.* New York: Monthly Review, 1961.

GALBRAITH, J. K. *The Affluent Society.* Boston: Houghton Mifflin, 1958.

MAGEE, BRIAN. *The New Radicalism.* New York: St. Martin's Press, 1963.

Party Manifestoes.

Socialist Union. *Twentieth Century Socialism*. Harmondsworth, Middlesex: Penguin Books, 1956.
TAWNEY, R. H. *The Acquisitive Society*. Gloucester, Mass.: Peter Smith, 1945.
————. *Equality*. New York: Barnes & Noble, 1964.

Chapter 3

BAUCHET, PIERRE. *Economic Planning: The French Experience*. Translated by DAPHNE WOODWARD. New York: Frederick A. Praeger, 1964.
COLE, M. and C. SMITH (eds.). *Democratic Sweden*. London: Routledge & Kegan Paul, 1938.
EINAUDI, BYÉ, and ROSSI. *Nationalization in France and Italy*. Ithaca, N.Y.: Cornell University Press, 1955.
ROBSON, W. A. *Nationalised Industry and Public Ownership*. London, Allen & Unwin, 1960.
SHANKS, MICHAEL (ed.). *The Lessons of Public Enterprise*. London: Jonathan Cape, 1963.
SHONFIELD, ANDREW. *Modern Capitalism*. London: Oxford University Press, 1965.
'Social Problems and Policies in Sweden,' *Annals of the American Academy of Political and Social Science*, 1938.

Chapter 4

CONDLIFFE, J. B. *The Welfare State in New Zealand*. London: Allen & Unwin, 1959.
ELTZ, SYLVIA. *Health and Pension Insurance in Sweden*. Swedish Institute, 1963.
HALL, M. PENELOPE. *The Social Services of Modern England*. London: Routledge & Kegan Paul, 1963.
RUGE, HERMAN. *Educational Systems in Scandinavia*. Scandinavia Universities, 1962.
TITMUSS, R. H. *Essays on the Welfare State*. London: Allen & Unwin, 1960.

Chapter 5

BERNSTEIN, EDUARD. *Evolutionary Socialism*. New York: Schocken Books, 1963.
CARTER, GWENDOLEN M. and J. H. HERZ. *Government and Politics in the Twentieth Century*. Rev. ed. New York: Frederick A. Praeger, 1965.

DURBIN, E. F. M. *Politics of Democratic Socialism.* London: Labour Book Service, 1940.
DUVERGER, MAURICE. *Political Parties.* New York: Science Editions, 1956.
LIPSET, SEYMOUR M. *Political Man: The Social Bases of Politics.* New York: Doubleday, 1959.
RUSTOW, D. A. *The Politics of Compromise.* Princeton, N.J.: Princeton University Press, 1955.

Chapter 6
BEEVER, R. COLIN. *European Unity and the Trade Union Movements.* Sythoff, 1960.
COOPER, JACK. *Industrial Relations: Sweden Shows the Way.* Fabian Society Research Series, 1963.
DARIN-DRABKIN, H. *The Other Society.* New York: Harcourt, Brace & World, 1963.
DIGBY, MARGARET. *The World Co-operative Movement.* London: Hutchinson University Library, 1960.
JOHNSTON, T. L. *Collective Bargaining in Sweden.* London: Allen & Unwin, 1963.
LUNDBERG, JOHN. *In Our Own Hands.* Sweden, 1962.
PELLING, HENRY. *A History of British Trade Unionism.* London: Macmillan, 1963.

Chapter 7
ANDERSON, PERRY (ed.). *Toward Socialism.* London: Fontana Library, 1965.
CROSLAND, C. A. R. *The Conservative Enemy.* New York: Schocken Books, 1963.
HALL, PETER. *London 2000.* London: Faber & Faber, 1963.
JAY, DOUGLAS. *Socialism in the New Society.* New York: St. Martin's Press, 1963.
ROBERTS, B. C. *National Wages Policy in War and Peace.* London: Allen & Unwin, 1958.
WILLIAMS, RAYMOND. *The Long Revolution.* New York: Columbia University Press, 1961.
WILSON, HAROLD. *The New Britain: Selected Speeches 1964.* Harmondsworth, Middlesex: Penguin Books, 1964.

Chapter 8

FITZSIMONS, M. A. *Foreign Policy of the British Labour Government*: 1945-1951. Notre Dame, Ind.: University of Notre Dame Press, 1953.

JOLL, JAMES. *The Second International*. London: Weidenfeld & Nicolson, 1955.

NOEL-BAKER, PHILIP. *The Arms Race*. Dobbs Ferry, N.Y.: Oceana Publications, 1959.

Socialist Union. *Socialism and Foreign Policy*. Book House, 1953.

Chapter 9

BLELLOCH, DAVID. *One Developing World*. Syracuse, N.Y.: Syracuse University Press, 1963.

BROCKWAY, FENNER. *African Socialism*. Chester Springs, Pa.: Dufour, 1963.

GALBRAITH, J. K. *Economic Development in Perspective*. Cambridge, Mass.: Harvard University Press, 1963.

HUNTER, GUY. *The New Societies of Tropical Africa*. New York: Frederick A. Praeger, 1964.

MYRDAL, G. *Beyond the Welfare State*. New Haven: Yale University Press, 1960.

ROSE, SAUL (ed.). *Politics in Southern Asia*. New York: St. Martin's Press, 1963.

STRACHEY, JOHN. *The End of Empire*. New York: Frederick A. Praeger, 1964.

Index

Adler, Viktor, 16
Advertising, 113–14
Algeria, 136
Anderson, Perry, *New Left Review*, 112n.
Arkwright, Richard, 2
Atlantic Charter, 135
Attlee, Clement, 25, 37, 68, 126, 127, 131, 135; on British Civil Service, 77; on Colonial independence, 134, 135; on individual freedom, 32; on Socialism in Sweden and New Zealand, 22; on war Coalition, 37, 38
Attwood, Thomas, 5
Australia, 1n., 3, 75, 79, 126
Australian Labour Party and Governments, 15, 23, 38, 102, 103, 145
Austria: coalition in, 76; difficulties of Democracy in, 69; party system in, 75; public ownership in, 44, 45, 47–8; Trade Unions in, 85
Austrian Socialist Party (SPÖ): ideology of, 11, 24, 74–5, 121; and local government, 79; opponents of Hitler, 68; in post-war Coalition, 38, 76; rise of, 16, 102, 145–6; structure of, 74–5
Automation, 102, 106–8, 111, 112

Baldwin, Stanley, 119
Bauchet, Pierre, *Economic Planning: The French Experience*, 52n.
Bebel, Ferdinand August, 25, 120
Belgium, 38, 102, 119, 132, 133, 136
Bernstein, Eduard, 13, 25, 67, 69; *Evolutionary Socialism*, 14n.
Bevan, Aneurin: on priorities, 36; on Health Service, 58
Beveridge Report, 37
Bevin, Ernest, 22, 36, 87, 118, 121
Bismarck, 9, 11, 15, 44
Blum, Léon, 24, 25
Boyle, Robert, 2
Brandt, Willi, 78
Branting, Hjalmar, 25, 124
Bright, John, 5, 10
British Chartist Movement, 10
British Labour Governments 1924 and 1929, 17, 21–2, 124–5, 129–30